CONCEPTUAL LEARNING

SIEGFRIED ENGELMANN

University of Illinois

Dimensions Publishing Co.

San Rafael, California

94903

EDITOR

Keith E. Beery
University of California
San Francisco Medical Center

ASSOCIATE EDITOR

Barbara D. Bateman
University of Oregon

DEDICATION
TO
SAMUEL A. KIRK

This is the year of Samuel A. Kirk's retirement from the Institute for Research on Exceptional Children at the University of Illinois.

History will record that Dr. Kirk was one of the major educational forces of the Twentieth Century. Although his energy has been directed toward assisting handicapped children in their learning and development, his work has already created an impact upon general education. This impact will grow in the coming years as we become more deeply aware that every child is unique and deserving of individualized instruction.

The Dimensions in Early Learning monograph series is dedicated, as a small token of appreciation, to this man whose name will take its place in education with those of Itard, Seguin, Binet, and Montessori . . . whose students will become the educational leaders of the Twenty-First Century.

CONTENTS

A SUMMARY OF ENGELMANN'S CONCEPTUAL LEARNING

By BARBARA BATEMAN

Siegfried Engelmann knows how to teach things to children and believes that doing so is a most urgent and important undertaking. Engelmann knows, as does every parent, that there are many times in a child's life when the things he needs to learn should be taught directly and efficiently. A child might eventually discover for himself, on an incidental learning basis, the rules for crossing streets safely. But we realize that this matter is too critical to be left to the child's own learning style and time. It might come too late or perhaps never. Engelmann believes that learning to think, reason, solve problems, and use language effectively is also highly urgent and that it is the business of teachers to efficiently and effectively manipulate the environment so that children are taught these things.

All of us who have watched the Bereiter-Engelmann program grow and have seen the children in the program become smarter and happier about themselves, stand in awe of the Engelmann-style teaching. We have seen Engelmann's techniques for teaching reading, arithmetic and language and we have marvelled. One of our big and haunting questions has been, "How?" How does Engelmann look with fresh eyes at content so badly fumbled by the rest of us and develop his own clear and precise teaching procedures?

This monograph is Engelmann's answer to how a master teacher derives his teaching procedures. The monograph is not easy reading, nor could it be. The following summary is an effort to simplify and highlight some of the main steps involved in the teacher's determination of how she is going to teach. Our deepest hope is that this summary will encourage the reader to explore the entire monograph. But even failing that, we believe Engelmann's message is so vital to the improvement of educational practices today that we willingly risk the dangers in summarizing another's work to bring to all our readers the "main gist" of this monograph. Mr. Engelmann has graciously allowed us to attempt this, even though it must distress him to see bare bones where he painted voluptuous figures. We have included examples which are not his and have omitted some points he stresses. Any distortions or inaccuracies are ours.

Overview

The monograph can be viewed in three parts. Chapter I—V describe the derivation of concept teaching procedures; Chapter VI presents the teaching of problem solving as an extension of the basic concept teaching procedures presented in the first section; Chapter VII describes the systematic teaching of persistence, positive self-image, acceptable classroom behavior, and a liking for school learning.

The first five chapters can be schematized as shown below. Following an introduction, Chapter II teaches us how to analyze the concept to be taught so that we derive from the analysis two things— the teaching routines or demonstrations to be done by the teacher and the tasks or tests to be performed by the children to demonstrate their learning. For example, when the teacher points to the letter m and says "this is m-m-m", that is part of the teaching routine; when she asks the children "is this m-m-m?" and they must reply, that is a task or test. Chapter III presents teacher routines and Chapter IV deals with tasks. The routines and tasks must be interwoven and sequenced into the total teaching programs as discussed in Chapter V.

Some of the major terms which Engelmann uses are included at the end of this summary for easy reference. This glossary is intended to alert the reader that terminology in this monograph is highly important.

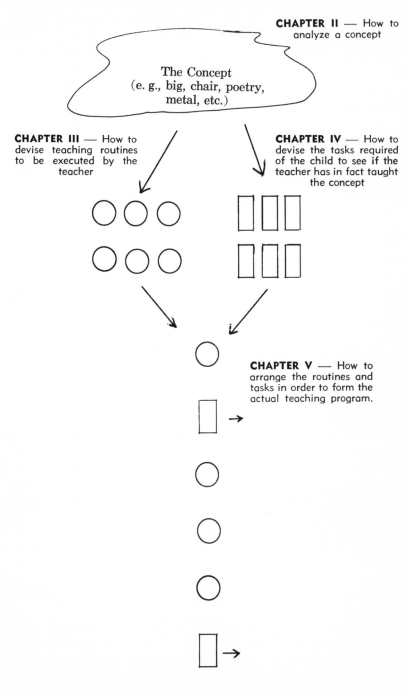

CHAPTER II — How to analyze a concept

The Concept
(e. g., big, chair, poetry, metal, etc.)

CHAPTER III — How to devise teaching routines to be executed by the teacher

CHAPTER IV — How to devise the tasks required of the child to see if the teacher has in fact taught the concept

CHAPTER V — How to arrange the routines and tasks in order to form the actual teaching program.

CHAPTER II: CONCEPT ANALYSIS

A concept is the set of characteristics shared by all those and only those instances in a particular set. Whatever it is that is true of all the red objects in the room and is true only of the red objects —that is the concept of *red*. If many farm animals were all together in the barnyard, the concept of *horse* would be comprised of all those things which could be observed about all the horses and only the horses.

Concepts are always dependent on the context or universe in which they are presented. The concept of *horse* as we would derive it in the barnyard would not be the same as we would use in a museum collection of fossil reconstructions of mammals much like our horses. The concept of metal as we use it in our everyday lives is very different from the concept of metal a laboratory scientist must use. Teachers must realize they are not only free to plan the context in which a concept will be taught, but that there isn't any other way to do it. The primary teacher knows that the concept of *living things* as she teaches it in context of rocks, desks and ceilings is not the same concept of living things that will be taught in a graduate biology course. And that is as it should be.

To analyze a concept so that we may teach it is to describe the concept in terms of the minimum set of essential discriminations the child must make in order to recognize that an instance is or is not a member of that concept set. The child is looking at pictures of many, many objects. What essential discriminations must he make in order to know whether a certain object is a *vehicle?* In all probability, "if people ride on it to get someplace" it's a vehicle. The analysis of the concept of *vehicle* reveals that the child must be taught to discriminate between things that people ride to get places and all other kinds of things (not vehicles). Notice that this analysis reveals the discrimination the child must make, but says nothing at all about how he is to demonstrate he is *making* it. The teacher might decide to have him point to all the vehicles and accept that as evidence he has learned the concept; or she might require him to write a 500 word essay on the features that distinguish vehicles from non-vehicles. The concept analysis reveals only the minimum discrimination to be made; it never dictates what response the child must make to show he has learned the concept.

To teach a concept we must teach the minimum discriminations the child must make to tell instances that do belong to that concept from instances that do not belong to it. Our analysis of the concept must reveal to us what these critical elements or discriminations really are. And it then is clearly obvious that what the critical elements are all depends on the context in which the concept is presented. If, for instance, we were to teach young children the concept of *war,* the critical element might be "groups of people fighting." We could demonstrate many scenes of groups variously engaged and have him point to the ones which depict war. In later years, the universe of instances presented might change from pictures of fighting and not fighting to verbal descriptions of treaties, resolutions, military maneuvers, etc., and the essential discrimination to be made might then change to whether the governing body of a given nation had or had not declared that nation to be at war.

CHAPTER III: TEACHING

Teaching consists of two components—the demonstrations the teacher performs to show the characteristics of concepts and the test or task the child must perform to demonstrate his understanding of the concept. Chapter 2 deals only with the teacher's demonstration —what she says and does to show the concept—although in practice these teaching routines and the tasks performed by the children are inseparable. Let us suppose that what the teacher wants to demonstrate is the concept of *m.* The initial analysis of *m* reveals that the critical discriminations the child must make are the configuration and the orientation in space. Size and color are irrelevant characteristics. The teacher must select the *way* she wants children to demonstrate they have learned to watch only for configuration and orientation. She might ask the children to draw a line under all the *m*'s. Or she might require them to verbally respond to each *m* by saying "*m-m-m.*" Clearly the latter response is more closely related to the reading task, so we would hope she would choose that task for the children.

This chapter deals with what the teacher must *do,* i.e., devising a routine so that the children will recognize all *m*'s and only *m*'s and can demonstrate this by whatever task she has selected and incorporated into the teaching procedure.

No concept can be taught by a single demonstration. Some children might learn it, but it was not taught. Below is a single demonstration of a ZAB.

What is a ZAB? It is impossible to tell, although some might guess correctly. The teacher must demonstrate by other instances, what are the essential elements in a ZAB.

These are ZABS:

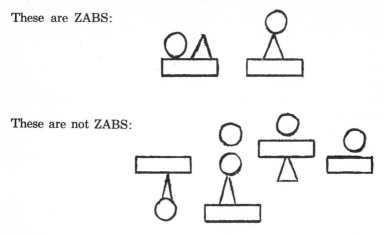

These are not ZABS:

The picture begins to emerge—all ZABS and only ZABS are comprised of one circle, one triangle, and one rectangle, with the rectangle on the bottom.

The teaching of a concept requires the presentation of both instances and not-instances. A teaching routine must be consistent with the concept being taught and *only* with that concept. If a teacher were to attempt to teach *red* by saying "This apple is red," the statement would be true, but it is totally inadequate because "red" as so presented could refer to any number of concepts. The child might conclude that *red* refers to round, to apple, to stem, or size, etc. The best presentation is one with the least potential for mis-rules and with a minimal memory load (e.g., five instances presented in one lesson requires less memory than five instances casually encountered over a period of a month).

In developing a presentation the teacher should concentrate on the *critical* discriminations the child must make. For instance, in teaching the small letter *h*, the height of the stem is the essential discrimination necessary to prevent confusion with the most similar and hence potentially confusing letter—*n*. In teaching a concept such as *heavy* it would be ideal to have several pairs of objects alike in every respect (size, color, shape, etc.) except weight. Rapid presentation of instances decreases the memory load and increases the ease with which discriminations are made.

Chapter IV: Tasks and Task Analysis

Tasks which the child must perform are an integral part of the teaching situation; otherwise, the teacher has no way of evaluating the effectiveness of the routine. If in teaching the concept of *on* the teacher has included the demonstration, "The ball is on the table", that would be part of the teaching *routine*. The corresponding *task* which requires the child to respond might be: "Put the ball on the table," or "Is the ball on the table?" or "Draw a picture of a ball on a table." The task always requires the child do something; the demonstration does not. The teacher must always select the task for the child to perform. It is not implied in the concept.

Tasks can be grouped into task classes, and we do not say the child understands the task until he has mastered an understanding of other tasks in that class. From the task "Put the ball in the box" we can construct a task class which would include "Throw the ball on the floor, place the cup over the dish, etc." Once this task class has been constructed, the class constitutes the real test of the child understanding.

Excellent suggestions and guidelines are given for legitimately reducing concepts to a teachable level of complexity and for constructing tasks that are fair.

Chapter V: Programming

Programming is the sequencing or the putting-in-the-best-order of the routines and tasks. The test of whether the material is programmed, as opposed to simply collated or compiled, is whether the teacher can correct a child's mistake by referring only to previous demonstrations. If she can, the material is programmed; if not, it is not programmed.

Efficient programming depends on recognizing that every concept we may wish to teach is at the same time a sub-concept within a larger concept. The most efficient teaching routine is one which simultaneously demonstrates the sub-concepts and also teaches the broader concept by virtue of the fact that the sub-concepts are treated the same way. For example, *wet* and *soft* are both concepts and they are both sub-concepts of the broad class of polars or opposites. If something is not wet, we know it is dry. If it is not soft, we know it is hard. We must teach *wet* and *soft* separately because they are different concepts, but similarly because they are both polar concepts. Therefore, the routine used is the same.

In programming properly we begin with a broad cluster of concepts such as those characteristics which reside in objects including color, position, size, shape, etc. The routine for teaching each must incorporate the fact that each of these characteristics resides in objects and requires sensory investigation. They can all be taught alike. The routine for presenting *big* is like the routine for presenting *red*. When the child learns the first concept he also has to learn the structure of the broader cluster of residual characteristics known by sensory investigation. This necessity for "double" learning during the first instance of a concept cluster results in the "sacrificial instance." The sacrificial instance requires the greatest learning and is the most poorly retained. The programmer may solve the problem of the sacrificial instance in 3 ways; use a trivial first instance that doesn't really matter to the total program; make the first instance easier (by experimentation it might be determined, e.g., that prepositions are easier than colors and "in" is the easiest of the prepositions); make the task required of the child easier.

Engelmann's first extended example of an efficient program demonstrates vividly how three concepts—linear equations, lever problems, and averages—are all instances of the broader concept of the equality rule. The same routines are used to teach all three. The program is used with five and six year olds, but the reaction of most adult readers is, "Oh, why didn't anybody ever teach me that before? Now I see what is really involved here."

The second extended program is that for teaching the concept of geological time. The basis for the routine is the principle of piling. When things are piled, they go this way ↑ . The program starts with this principle because it can readily demonstrated in everyday life, just as lever problems were taught first in the preceding program because they can be compellingly demonstrated.

Chapter VI: Problem Solving

Problem solving does not form a class distinct from other concept teaching. Problems are complex tasks and are taught as such. Engelmann suggests that much of the confusion surrounding the teaching of problem solving arises from ambiguity regarding the *intent* of the task. For example, the familiar water-transfer problems involve the child seeing water transfered from one container to a differently shaped container and then making a judgment as to whether the *amount* of water has changed. A very adequate program could be designed to teach children to solve this and all other water-as-fixed units problems. But naive critics might object that children taught by this program were not able to *also* solve problems involving the flattening of a ball of clay into a large pancake and judgments regarding constancy of mass.

Engelmann's point is that if the intent of the problem-solving routine is to teach the broader concept of *compensating changes,* it will require a different routine than would be used for the narrower concept of *water-as-fixed units.* Only when the intent is clarified, can an appropriate program be generated. But the broad concept would be taught just as explicitly and directly. There is no reliance on magical or mysterious "transfer" of what is taught to a new situation.

Teaching "problem-solving" is teaching concept clusters. Six rules are presented for programming the teaching of a concept cluster:

1. Specify the cluster precisely.

2. Develop a routine which treats all instances of the cluster in the same way.

3. Choose demonstration instances from the cluster, selecting them so that no mis-rules are induced.

4. Use cues in the demonstration that facilitate transfer to a variety of tasks.

5. Begin with demonstrations that are valid and real to the child.

6. Construct total routines which are adequate and efficient.

Chapter VII: Programming Reinforcement

When a child is taught a particular task he must learn three things: (1) the concept being taught; (2) the rules for responding to the concept; and (3) the rule that responding is worthwhile. If he isn't taught both the second and third we can never know whether he learned the concept. In order for the child to want to respond, the teacher must use reinforcement appropriately. Reinforcement should be used non-contingently during the demonstrations by the teacher and contingently in structuring the tasks to be performed by the child.

The teacher must remember that every instance of teaching teaches the child something about himself and learning situations, in addition to whatever content concepts are being taught. This is unavoidable because every instance of teaching is an instance of the concept of "child as a learner." The child who fails in several instances is being *taught* that he is a failure in school learning situations! Concepts about the teacher, about the material, the importance of school work, and about the child's adequacy are taught just like any other concepts—instances are presented and rules formulated.

Content-independent concepts ("I am smart", "I can get it if I try," "School is fun", "Arithmetic is useful", etc.) must be *programmed* in such a way that they do not distract from the teaching of the concept and so that the instances of the content-independent concept are clear and unequivocal. The pay-off for making the required responses must be real to the child and have pay-off value for him. Some things adults think will function as pay-offs for children do not actually do so.

When the teacher is using reinforcement in the teaching demonstration she should use it non-contingently. In other words, reinforcers are built into the demonstration so that children will like and attend to the demonstration. The demonstration should contain elements that are pleasurable for children (objects they find interesting; funny story themes, etc.) but which are not so strong that the children will focus on them to the exclusion of the content concept being taught.

The key to a dynamic presentation is that the teacher's behavior should be very predictable *within* routines and quite unpredictable *between* routines. The displays the children are watching should change at least every minute, the teacher should use dramatic changes of pace, and should include inflections and rhythms the children enjoy.

Specific suggestions and routines are presented for teaching these content independent concepts: "What is learned is useful; therefore I should learn it because I will need it"; "I'll succeed if I keep working and trying"; "I can do it" (self-confidence in school situations); and rules for acceptable classroom behavior.

GLOSSARY

Concept Analysis:

description of a concept which (1) tells us the minimum essential features of that concept which must be taught and (2) does this in such a way that we can derive environmental manipulations or teaching demonstrations from our analysis.

Concept Analyst, Task Analyst, Programmer:

the person, usually the teacher (unless she has access to previously prepared *complete* guides), responsible for analyzing concepts, deriving teaching demonstrations and routines, devising tasks, and sequencing tasks and demonstrations. These skills should constitute a major part of every teacher's professional tools. The choice of concept to be taught is traditionally made by "curriculum planner", but seldom are the concepts adequately described. In effect, the teacher is most often required to make the selection.

General Function:

when two concepts differ from each other in a number of significant ways (e.g., horses and dogs differ in size, configuration, feet, etc.), they are said to have a general function with respect to each other.

Specific Function:

when two concepts differ in only one critical characteristic they serve a specific function with respect to each other. To change an octagon to a decagon requires only one conversion (the addition of two more sides, with the concomitant angle changes), so octagons have a specific function with respect to decagons.

Concept:

a set of characteristics which differentiate a group of instances (events, objects, relationships, etc.) from all other instances presented. The concept may change as the setting in which it is presented changes.

Class: concept.

Positive Instance or Concept Instance:

an example which *is* a case of the concept under discussion. A terrier is a positive instance of *dog*. The black ball (⭘ ⬤ ⭘) is a positive instance of *middle*.

Negative or NOT Instance:

an example which is *not* a case of the concept under discussion. A mouse is a *not* instance of dog.

Teaching Routine:

the behaviors (verbal and gestural) the teacher does to demonstrate to the children the essence of the concept—the way in which all the instances may be treated the same. In a sense, the routine is the teacher's rendering of her "script."

Task:

what the child does to demonstrate that he has learned the concept. The tasks or tests in a teaching situation always involve a response from the child. The teacher's routine does not involve the child's response, e.g., the teacher may say, "The book is *on* the table", "The ball is *on* the floor," etc., as part of her routine. When she asks Johnny "Is the spoon *on* the plate?" she is presenting a task or test to the child.

Signal or Task Convention

the cues the child must know in order to make the desired responses to indicate he has learned the concept. For instance, in learning the concept of *red* he must also learn to respond to such signals as "Point to the red one" or "Put an X on the red ones" or "Say 'red'."

Discovery:

the highly structured process by which the child extracts the concept from the instances presented.

ACKNOWLEDGMENT

I am grateful to Dr. H. S. Harris, who demonstrated to me rather forcefully several eons ago when I was a student working towards my college degree, that philosophy lives within other fields. Philosophy is not a thing; it is the fabric of science and history, architecture and education. Dr. Harris showed me, further, that the goal of philosophy within these fields is to offer alternative explanations. If an alternative explanation accounts for the "facts" and has functional advantages over other explanations, one must acknowledge that explanation, regardless of how he may feel about it. The alternative-explanation principle has greatly influenced my thinking, and I hope that the present outline is a favorable reflection of Dr. Harris' teachings.

CHAPTER I

CONCEPTS AND CONCEPT BEHAVIOR

Concepts are both interesting and elusive to the psychological investigator—interesting because they are there in the real world and elusive because they are difficult to abstract, measure, quantify, and discuss. The general solution to the problem has been to try to reduce them to *behavior*. Instead of specifying what concepts are, investigators have talked about concept behavior. Their goal is quite the same as that of the present outline—to find out what concepts are so that we can instruct teachers to teach them more effectively. These investigators have concluded that the best way to find out what they are is to study how they are learned. One's first reaction may be to note that this approach is about as logical as trying to find out what mathematical principles are by observing the ways in which people learn mathematics. Obviously, what people learn is correlated with what they are taught. Similarly, what people learn about concepts is correlated with what they are taught.

However, the problem is not that simple when one deals with concepts. Facts about how children learn concepts certainly have a potential influence on how concepts should be taught. If it is true that children tend to learn concepts more readily when instances of the concept are presented with a short time interval between instances, a teaching presentation should be designed to take advantage of this fact. This is an empirical fact. It cannot be derived from a study of concepts. It derives from a study of children. The fact that the children cannot consistently learn a concept unless there is more than one instance presented, however, is not an empirical fact. It is an analytical fact. It derives from an analysis of concepts, not from empirical studies. We can conduct empirical studies that demonstrate the "truth" of our concept analysis, but these studies are justified only if one supposes that children know concepts before they are taught concepts. The studies would then be able to demonstrate that children do not have concept foresight. The possibility of deriving strong analytical statements from empirical investigations, however, is slight. It is like trying to demonstrate that a particular object has the properties of an apple by demonstrating that a statistically significant number of people agree that the object is an apple. In fact, the object may be a pear and all of the people sampled may be morons.

A number of studies in concept usage and formation have been conducted and generally these are consistent with the analysis provided in the present outline. However, note that this outline, for the most part, does not derive in any way from the evidence. It derives from an analysis of concepts and from the unique problems associated with translating concepts into tasks and into teaching demonstrations. Empirical studies do not "confirm" the analysis.

The present outline is also based on psychological principles. The primary ones are:

1. A living organism has a limited memory.

2. A living organism can learn: (a) to group things that share a set of characteristics; and (b) to use the same response for all of the instances in the group.

The secondary psychological principles relate to general operations that make tasks more effective, especially in the area of reinforcement. However, these principles are strictly secondary. Effective programs do not derive from psychological principles or analyses of responses and stimuli. While it is possible to construct programs from a behavioral-analysis standpoint, it is usually difficult to specify how the program derived from the analysis or why any of a range of programs would not satisfy the stipulations imposed by the program. This problem is discussed more fully in Chapter 4.

In summary, this outline represents something of a fresh start. It probably presents not one new idea, but hopefully it arranges ideas in an order that establishes priorities and guidelines for analyzing concepts, translating them into demonstrations, testing the child's concept knowledge, and programming a series of concepts into a "program". The analysis represents a fresh start because it does not try to reduce concepts to behavior. It doesn't confuse a concept with learning a concept; nor does it confuse a concept with the tasks that are designed to test it or behavior that is consistent with it.

The foregoing discussion is not designed to impugn those who have conducted both useful and interesting experiments on how children learn concepts. The reader is encouraged to read about some of the studies that have been done, especially in the area of concept formation. Until recently, it has been difficult for a reader to go to the library and find a book that outlines both what kind of work has been done and what some of the more important psychological and analytical issues are. Lyle Bourne's 1966 book *Human Conceptual Behavior* provides a very concise introduction and overview. It is unfortunate that some of the experiments described in it have had such a meager impact on other areas of psychological research.

Perhaps the psychologist who has made the most concerted attempt to get outside of the organism and analyze the tasks that they are trying to learn is Gagne. Perhaps his most interesting work is *The Conditions of Learning* (1965). This book will acquaint the reader with an approach for arranging tasks and deriving teaching sequences from the analysis.

A note of apology. Throughout this outline, reference is made to principles of programming and the conveyance of information through examples. The reader will probably discover long before he has finished the outline that the author has scrupulously violated every principle he sets forth. The author is aware of his violations. He could excuse himself by saying that space prevents the kind of presentation that would unambiguously convey all of his ideas. Instead, he will be honest and say that he doesn't know how to do it in the allotted space.

CHAPTER II

CONCEPT ANALYSIS

Concept analysis and the construction of programs to teach a particular set of concepts is a strange combination of analysis and the application of psychological principles. The combination is strange because the act of teaching is unique. Basically, it is a process of manipulation. The idea behind any teaching program is to change the person receiving instruction, not in any direction, but in a very specific way. Since teaching is a manipulative art or science, the products of analysis must always allow for translation into specific tasks and procedures. They must always be expressed in terms of how-to-do-it principles. Not all of the answers about how to do it can be distilled from an analysis of a concept. For example, the analysis will not tell the analyst anything about the relative difficulty of a particular task. It will tell him simply that a task that satisfies a particular concept requirement must be introduced. To find out something about the difficulty of the task, the analyst must try out the task and see whether it works smoothly. On the try-out level, the analyst may find it useful to refer to certain principles of psychology. These may provide him with clues about how to set up the tasks so that the children will be "motivated", will make fewer errors, and will become more able to work independently. However, most of the principles outlined in this monograph "override" psychological principles. They guide the development of a teaching sequence. They imply the tasks that must be taught. The principles of psychology do not. They apply only after a task or series has been identified. The fact that some of the principles derived from concept analysis agree with psychological principles is not actually a tribute to psychological principles. It is evident that many of the questions that are asked by psychologists do not have anything to do with psychology at all, but deal with the structure of the concepts. These questions can be answered more efficiently by referring to concept analysis than to empirical studies.

5

I bring up this point because so much of the work in the study of concept formation is based on psychological theories, which are at best, tangential to the principles that most productively describe certain learning phenomona from the standpoint of the teacher. For example, the question of "generalization" is usually treated as a psychological question. If one is interested in individual differences in generalization style, then the question is probably within the domain of psychology. But if one is interested in the "laws" that govern generalization (assuming that skills learned in a particular setting can legitimately generalize to another setting) one is not talking about psychology but about the structure of concepts as they relate to teaching. This is not to say that concept analysis represents a pure form of analysis. Quite the contrary. At its base is a certain artistic ability, and woven into its fabric are fragments of psychology. However, the fabric is not one of psychology. It is one of concept analysis.

The procedure outlined on the following pages can be sketched as a four-stage process. First, a concept is analyzed; then a series of teaching demonstrations is developed to satisfy the requirements of the concept analysis; next, tasks are developed to test the effectiveness of the teaching; finally, a series of demonstrations and tests are sequenced to form a program. The analysis of the concept discloses what kind of discriminations the child must learn to make—what basic rule he must learn. If the concept is the color *red,* he must learn the basic rule that a certain hue on the surface of an object is red—not green, or yellow. The basic discrimination he must make is between things that are red and things that are not red. Our analysis tell's us this. However, our analysis tells us nothing about how to structure a teaching sequence for inducing a set of responses that willl let us know that the child has learned the discrimination. We therefore move into the second stage of the analysis—teaching. To teach the discrimination, we must teach the child a rule. We must demonstrate what redness is in such a way that he will have a basis for learning to discriminate between red things and things that are not red. We must make up tasks, and we must order these tasks in a broader instructional program so that the entire sequence is efficient. We can work out such a sequence without ever looking at a child.

The Analysis of a Concept

A concept analysis is a procedure for describing a concept in relevant terms; that is, *terms that will translate into specific manipulation of environmental variables.* This point is extremely important but often difficult to appreciate. In order to evaluate a particular theory, one must look at the uses to which the theory will

6

be put. A theory may be perfectly adequate for some uses and inadequate for other purposes. The theory, in other words, must be more than descriptively accurate. It must be designed so that it translates into the units of action that will be employed by a practioner. We could describe a bumper of a car in terms of its chemical elements. This description might be perfectly accurate, but it would be relatively useless to an automobile designer, who looks at the same bumper in terms of function and design, not in terms of chemical elements. Stated differently, two bumpers might be described in exactly the same terms according to an analysis of chemical composition. Both may have the same ratio of carbon to iron molecules, and so forth. Yet one of these bumpers may be acceptable to a designer and the other may be unacceptable. His design was not made on the basis of chemistry, but on appearance. What constitutes an adequate description for the chemist or the metallurgist does not constitute an adequate description for him. Still other people who are involved in producing automobiles may look at the bumper in still another way. The engineer may be concerned with weight and cost, bulkheading and finish. The bumper for him is not adequately described either in terms of "design" or chemical composition.

There are no theoretical descriptions that operate in the abstract. *All are geared to particular practitioners.* For that reason, we must look to the practitioner to decide whether or not a particular theory or set of procedural rules allows him to make the kinds of decisions he must make. The ideal description for a teacher or educator allows him to make very specific statements about how to teach concepts and about methods for solving problems. We cannot simply decide that a particular theory or description is "adequate" because is provides a full and accurates description. The description H_2O is not a comprehensive description of water; it is only comprehensive when one is making a particular set of decisions. It does not contribute to a great many of the decisions a physicist in fluid mechanics must make or to the decisions a poet who is describing water must make.

We can describe concepts in a number of ways, just as we can describe water in a number of ways. The only way we will be assured of constructing a description that will be useful for particular purposes, however, is to look at those purposes—in the present case, to look at teaching. Teaching is a manipulative science or art. The teacher does not manipulate by using drugs or by physically changing the learner. Rather, the teacher changes the learner only through the manipulation of environmental variables. He presents stimuli. He talks, he praises, he shows things to the learner, he requires responses. Only through the manipulation of environmental variables can he produce change. Our description of concepts, therefore, must imply specific manipulation of environmental variables. The word "specific" is extremely important because a teacher never operates in a general way. He doesn't "teach red". Rather, he presents specific things and uses specific statements. Was the nature of these demonstrations and statements implied by his "theory" or did they spring from some other source? According to what criteria did he select the objects to be presented? What principles influenced his use of language? These are the critical questions. If a theory implies simply teaching red or even breaking the teaching into "small steps", the theory is mute on important questions that make one teaching situation different from another.

Furthermore, the act of teaching is premised on the idea that there are absolute criteria of performance. Teaching implies specific objectives. An objective may be to teach children to read. The assumption is that there are ways of manipulating environmental variables that will induce "reading behavior" in children. A particular type of manipulation is successful if it teaches children to read. It is not successful if it does not teach children to read, *regardless of what else it may teach them.* After being exposed to a program that is intended to teach reading, the children may be able to handle quadratic equations. Even so, the program is a failure. The children cannot read. Unless we adhere to the stipulation that a program must be evaluated primarily in terms of what it is designed to teach, we open the door on the possibility of programs being introduced because they "may" teach an unspecified skill. "I don't know what this program teaches, but it must be good for something."

Stated differently, our description of concepts must take account of the fact that environmental manipulations are designed to produce particular outcomes. In other words, our description must not imply just any type of environmental manipulation. It must imply the type of environmental manipulation that will assure us of achieving particular objectives. Our analysis and description of concepts, what they are and how to program them, is based on the notion that children are taught, not that children learn. We are not denying that children learn (just as we would not deny that water is H_2O). For the purposes of the present analysis, however, we must express learning in such a way that we can produce it. This means that the focus is on what we do—how we manipulate the environmental variables to produce *desired* changes. If we focus on the child's learning, we will focus on an irrelevant aspect of the problem. Since our objective is to describe teaching—not learning—our basic assumption is that children are taught. We must rephrase all observations of "learning" to observations of "teaching", even though this convention may seem uncomfortable to us. *Only if we limit our description to those aspects of the total learning-teaching situation over which we have control, can we hope to construct an efficient description.* And a teacher has control only over teaching—over manipulating environmental variables to produce specific, desired changes in behavior.

What is a Concept?

A concept is a set of characteristics that is shared by all instances in a particular set and only by these instances.

In many respects, this is a strange description of concept. The notion of concept often refers to a person's behavior. We say, "He's got the concept of bigness," or "She doesn't have the concept of red." Yet, our description makes no reference to whether or not anybody has a particular concept. Nor does it mention anything about words. And it doesn't imply that concepts are absolute. According to this description, a concept is a function of the set of instances that is presented. The concept may change as the composition of the set changes. For example, if we make up a set that includes all of the dogs in the world and all of the horses in the world, the concept *dog* is the set of characteristics that all of the dogs have that none of the horses have. We note that dogs have paws, and that dogs are "small" and "light". Note that we must limit ourselves to those characteristics that are shared only by all dogs. We cannot make reference to ears, number of legs, warm-bloodedness, tails, etc., because horses share these characteristics. Note also that some of the characteristics that we observe as being shared only by all dogs cannot be expressed verbally. We observe that dogs have dogness configuration, but we cannot put this observation into words very handily.

According to our description of concept, we can change the concept, dog, by changing the composition of the set of instances. For example, we can add mice to the set of instances. Our concept changes. Now "smallness" and "lightness" are not characteristics that are shared only by all dogs. If we add lions to the set of instances, our concept of dog changes again. We can no longer make reference to paws. If we include all known animals our concept of dog would be quite different from the one obtained when the set of instances included only dogs and horses.

Our description of a concept allows us to specify the minimum set of essential discriminations that a learner must make to avoid confusing instances of a concept with instances that do not satisfy the concept requirements. If a child is to be taught the concept "dog" in relation to a set of instances that includes dogs and horses, we can specify the characteristics of the instances the child must attend to—the configuration, the size, the presence or absence of paws, etc. Since these are the characteristics that distinguish a dog from a horse, these are the characteristics that must be attended to if the child is to learn the discrimination. Note, however, that the child does not have to attend to all of the characteristics that are shared only by all dogs. He can learn to attend to any one of them. What this means is that there are a number of choices that could be made in a program to teach naive subjects to discriminate between dogs and horses. The programmer may choose to teach only the paw discrimination or only the size discrimination. There are choices in programming because any characteristic that is shared only by all dogs will allow one to distinguish between dogs and other members of the set.

We can look at the problem another way. Let's assume that any concept can be converted into any other concept. Let's assume that we could, by changing the characteristics of dogs, convert them into horses. What would we have to change? We would have to change the size of the animal, the general configuration, the paws, etc. If we have to change a number of characteristics to achieve the conversion, *the concept dog has a general function with respect to the concept horse.* No single change will achieve the conversion. This means that no single change is critical to the discrimination. Various characteristics or combinations of characteristics are sufficient to prevent confusion among the instances. If we were to try to convert police dogs into wolves, on the other hand, our conversation would be very specific. The primary shared characteristics of all police dogs that is not shared by any wolves is that police dogs bark. The conversion from a police dog to a wolf would therefore involve a change in a single characteristic. *When a change in only a single characteristic (or several characteristics) is needed to convert one concept into another, the concepts are said to have a specific function with respect to each other.* A specific function implies that the child must learn to attend to a specific characteristic if he is to avoid confusing instances of the concept with other instances in the set. Therefore, the programmer does not have the choices in programming that are available to him when concepts have a general function with respect to each other. The programmer must now teach a critical discrimination, because this is the discrimination that sets the concept instances apart from other instances.

Our description of concept allows us to give a relatively precise description of what psychologists sometimes refer to when they say that stimuli are similar. When we say that all dogs are similar, what do we mean? Do we mean that they look alike or that they are the same size? We mean that they share certain characteristics which are not shared by other instances of the set that is presented to the

10

learner. Dogs are similar because they share a set of characteristics. Instances of the concept *over* share a certain set of characteristics which are shared only by all instances of *over*. Our description also allows us to make statements about the possible confusion of concept instances with other instances.

The more specific the function a concept has with respect to another concept, the greater the possibility of confusion. Elephants, from almost every angle, are not easily confused with other animals, because elephants have a number of characteristics that are not shared by other animals. If there were an animal that looked like an elephant in every respect except that this animal did not have a trunk, the possibility of confusion would increase. Elephants would have a specific function with respect to these animals. The discrimination between elephant and these animals might still be learned with relative ease, however, because the presence of a trunk obviously changes the appearance of the animal. If there were a third animal that looked like an elephant but had a little fork at the end of its trunk, elephants would have a specific function with respect to this animal. The steps that we would take to convert an elephant into this animal would be much smaller than the steps we would take to convert an elephant-like-animal-without-a-trunk. Since the steps would be smaller and more specific, we would predict that naive subjects would have more difficulty learning to discriminate between elephants and forked-trunked animals than they would learning to discriminate between elephants and trunkless elephants. Our subjects would have to focus on a more specific characteristic than they would in learning to discriminate between elephants and trunkless elephants.

Note that our explanation makes no assumption about the absolute degree of difficulty that a subject would have in learning a discrimination. It merely implies that a discrimination becomes more difficult as the steps involved in converting concept instances into instances of another concept become fewer and more specific.

Classes

Things are often classified together. For example, dogs, cats, zebras, are often classified as mammals, as animals, or as living things. Each class designation is simply a regrouping of the intances.

If we had everything in the world—all events, objects, and relationships—included in a set, we could devise many "groupings" or classes. However, each class is simply a concept. We could group the things according to whether or not they are mammals. This is simply another way of saying that all mammals have a set of characteristics

11

that is not shared by any non-mammal. Grouping the instances according to whether or not they are living things is another way of saying that there is a concept, living things, and that every instance of this concept has a set of characteristics that is not shared by any non-living thing. If things share a set of characteristics that is not shared by other instances in the total set of instances or universe, a concept is defined.

If this idea seems strange, consider the concept *chair*. It is a class of things that have a set of shared characteristics. We should emphasize the word *set*. If the instances in the universe that is given include chairs, couches, and beds, the concept of *chair* would be these characteristics:

    a) designed to accommodate one person (to rule out couch)

    b) in a bent-knee sitting position with back supported (to rule out bed).

Instances of the concept *chair* must satisfy both of these requirements, not merely one of them. An object designed to accommodate people in a sitting position may be a couch, not a chair; an object designed to accommodate one person may not be a couch but a bed. The concept is not described in terms of specific things, but rather in terms of essential characteristics of a class of things. Any object that satisfies these characteristics is included in the class. Just as furniture is a class, chair is a class, and so is armchair, paisley-print overstuffed armchair, and so forth. With few exceptions, concepts are classes. It is possible to arrange these classes so that they are "hierarchical" or "coordinate", according to the characteristics they share. But we must always come back to the characteristics —the characteristics shared by the concept instances and the characteristics of the other instances in the universe that is presented.

Words and Concepts

Concept words sometimes become confused with concepts. The concept *adjective* would include words that share a certain set of characteristics. But the concept *red* or the concept *chair* would not include words. The concept red would include instances of red things and the concept chair would include objects that satisfy the concept requirements for chair. The words that we use in connection with such concepts as *red* and *chair* are simply signals that tell us, in an abbreviated way, that we are referring to things that share certain characteristics. Words used to refer to concepts other than language concepts (concepts of syntax, grammar, etc.) are independent concepts. This fact can be demonstrated quite easily. If a word is an essential characteristic of the concept instances, then it would be impossible to (a) substitute that word for another word, or (b) demonstrate awareness of the concept without using the word.

People who speak languages other than English do not use the word *red* to refer to the set of characteristics we refer to with the word *red*. Some people use the word *rot;* others use the word *rouge.* Yet, all refer to the same set of characteristics. Furthermore, we could attach any signal we wish—verbal or nonverbal—to demonstrate awareness of the concept red. We could teach children to identify red things by saying "green", by clapping, by pointing, or by saying, "Frack." Conversely, if children consistently identify red things with the same signal, we could conclude that they had been taught the *concept* red. The word is not the concept and is not a characteristic of the concept.

The Testing Specifications Implied by Concept Analysis

A concept is a set of characteristics that is shared only by the concept instances. The test that is implied by an anlysis of a concept is simply: Can a child demonstrate that he has been taught to discriminate the appropriate set of characteristics?

Note that the test is general. The person who has been taught a concept should be able to give *some* kind of demonstration that he can distinguish between instances, but a particular type of performance is not specified. This point is both important and somewhat paradoxical. If a child has been taught the concept *chair,* he should be able to pass a test in which he is required to distinguish between chairs and the other instances in the universe. Ultimately, the test will involve performance of some kind. There is no way to administer a test without specifying a particular kind of performance; yet, no particular kind of performance is implied by the concept. What is implied by the concept is the kind of "discrimination" that the child must make, not the responses that he is to produce or the signal to respond that is presented. If an essential characteristic of chair is "a back", a child must be able to discriminate between objects that are identical in every respect except for the back. And he should be able to indicate that the object without the back is not a chair. If an essential characteristic of chair is that it accommodates one person, the child should be able to indicate that an object identical to armchair in every respect except for the number of people it accommodates is not a chair. He should be able to handle each of the shared characteristics in this way.

The test should focus on the specific functions of a particular concept. The general functions do not have to be tested as thoroughly simply because a general function provides the learner with redundant information. It is possible for one to confuse a police dog with regular geometric figures, such as triangles, but the chances are slim that such confusion would result, simply because the concept police dog has a general function with respect to geometric figures. We would have to change many of the observable characteristics of a police dog to transform it into any kind of geometrical figures. *And we would have to perform a similar set of transformations for any geometric figure we chose.* Most of the steps involved in transforming a police dog into a circle would be the same as those involved in changing a police dog into a square. We would first have to change a solid object into a line. We would have to eliminate all of the "inflections" in the outline of the dog. We would have to eliminate the parts that are observable in a dog. Note that all of these changes must be made. Each characteristic of a dog must be eliminated. Since there are many such characteristics, the possibility of being able to discriminate between a dog and a geometric shape is increased. The person learning the discrimination does not have to rely on a single characteristic for his information. He can rely on any characteristic (or any combination) that would have to be changed before a dog would look like a circle. The test that is implied is always a test of a particular concept, which means a particular range of instances in a particular universe of instances. If the universe consists of chairs and couches, the child is not tested on a concept that derives from a universe of chairs, couches, stools, and footstools. Perhaps the principle that is most often violated in education is that a concept must test that particular concept.

The concept implies tests of irrelevant characteristics as well as tests of essential characteristics. Color, height of back, number of legs, and presence and absence of arms are not among the characteristics shared only by chairs. (We cannot convert a chair into a nonchair by changing the color or the height of the back, but we can change it simply by widening it.) The child should be able to demonstrate that he understands these characteristics to be irrelevant. For example, if he is presented with chairs that are identical in all respects except for the presence of arms, will he indicate that both are chairs?

Implications

A programmer has a number of choices available to him. He can set up the universe of instances as he chooses. He can select the responses to be used in a test as he chooses. But once he has identified the universe of instances, a test is implied. The programmer has no choice in this matter. He cannot choose another test. He cannot present a simplified version of the test. For example, he cannot select a universe of instances that includes chairs, couches, and beds, and then test his children only on whether they can discriminate between chairs and dogs. He cannot test them only on their ability to use the word *chair*. He must test them on the discriminations that are implied by the concept.

The fact that a test is implied by a concept is simply another way of saying that if certain characteristics are essential to a concept, a child must be taught about these characteristics, regardless of what else he is taught. A child who is taught the word "flot" for identifying chairs is taught a different response than the child who claps every time a chair is presented. But both children must be able to demonstrate that they have been taught the *same thing about what chairs are*. Unless they can provide this demonstration, we cannot say that they have the concept *chair*.

This point is sometimes not appreciated by programmers. Some investigators suggest that if a terminal behavior is specified, one can write a program that will shape the appropriate responses. A programmer should not accept the premise that certain responses are given. Concepts are given. Once they are given, tests are given. Only now does the question of behavior enter into the sequence. To look at the problem of programming from the starting point of behavior is often to develop poor programs.

Questions about the range of the concept instances, the instances that are included in the universe, and the set of shared characteristics that must be tested now become secondary to responses and specific stimuli.

Teaching Specifications Implied by Concept Analysis

Just as the test is generally implied by an analysis of the concept, teaching specifications are implied by the concept. These are not specific techniques, items, questions, or the like. *These are specifications about what must be taught.* The teaching specifications can be expressed as follows: the teaching must account for inducing those discriminations on which the child will be tested. A teaching sequence designed to teach children to distinguish between chairs, couches, and beds must account for "perfect" performances on the test. Before the child is exposed to the program, he cannot make the discriminations that are implied by the test. After he has been through the program, it is assumed that the child will perform perfectly on the test. What happens to change the child? How is he taught that the height of a chair's back is an irrelevant characteristic? How was he taught that the presence or absence of a back is a relevant characteristic? The process by which the child learns the "rule" about the concept is either mysterious or it is not. If it is, there can be no precise technology of teaching. If it is not, the teaching sequence must teach the rule—must demonstrate which characteristics are relevant and which are irrelevant to the concept.

When the relationship between teaching and concept analysis is made explicit, teaching sequence can be evaluated more precisely. We know what the program must teach. We know that the goal of the program is to teach the structure of the concept. If a programmer does not account for all facets of the concept structure, we don't have to run empirical tests to say that the program is inadequate. An examination of the program will disclose its inadequacies.

Summary

There are no concepts in the abstract. The concept, *metal,* exists only in relationship to a specific universe of instances. If we never expect a person to discriminate between metals and non-metals in a laboratory situation, we would not introduce instances of non-metals that are discriminable from metals only through some kind of laboratory test. A child will be expected to use a concept only in a certain set of situations. We must start with these situations if we are to discover what kind of discriminations he must learn to avoid confusion. We may, at a later time, expand the universe of instances, in which case the concept will change, because the set of characteristics that is shared only by concept instances will change.

A given concept is analyzed by referring to the observable characteristics of the positive instances of the concept in a given universe. If the positive instances comprise a single concept, there is something we can note about these instances that cannot be noted about any of the other instances. That something is the concept. It is the essential characteristics that distinguishes the concept instances from other instances. This rule holds whether the concept is "poetry", "beauty", "under", or "independent clause". If one specifies the universe and if one is actually dealing with a concept, there is a unique set of shared characteristics.

Once a concept has been analyzed, testing specifications and teaching specifications are implied. If a set of shared characteristics is shared only by the concept instances, a person has the concept only if he can demonstrate, through some kind of performance, that he can distinguish between instances that have the set of shared characteristics and instances that do not.

The teaching specifications that are implied by the concept analysis are based on the assumption that if a child can pass a test that is implied by a concept, he has been taught how to "pass the test".

16

This means that he has been taught each of the discriminations included in the testing specifications.

The analysis of the concept provides us both with specifications of what test the child must be able to pass and a method for judging programs designed to teach concepts. Unless the teaching accounts for the discriminations the child must make to pass the test, the sequence is inadequate.

CHAPTER III

TEACHING

The objective of teaching is to somehow give the child concepts by showing him the sets of shared characteristics that comprise these concepts. The dilemma of teaching is that it is impossible to give him concepts directly. A teacher cannot say, "Here's the concept," and give it to the child. At best he can describe the concept with words, but not all concepts can be described verbally, and a verbal description often assumes a very sophisticated knowledge of language, which the child may not have.

Often a teacher must somehow demonstrate the concept. To show a child that different instances of a concept share a set of characteristics and that these characteristics can be referred to with a word, the teacher often has to present many instances of the concept. He then presents "not-instances" to show the child instances that do *not* share the essential characteristics. Generally, he presents an instance at a time, which means that some time may be required before he has presented a sufficient number of instances for the child to see what the invarient characteristics are that are shared by the concept instances.

Another feature of the teaching situation is that the teacher must receive feedback from the child. He must see whether the child has learned the concept. He cannot observe the child's concept any more than the child can observe the teacher's. Testing is therefore a necessary part of any teaching demonstration. The test is in the form of a *task* or series of tasks. The greater the number of tasks the teacher uses, the greater the amount of feedback about the child's performance he receives. If he tests children once a week, he will receive less "process information" than if he tests them every few minutes.

This chapter deals only with a phase of teaching—the demonstration that is designed to show the children what the concept is. The following chapter will discuss the other component of teaching, the test or *task* and its relationship to the teaching demonstration and the concept being taught. In actual practice, demonstrations are not separable from testing. A teacher must "diagnose" the children in terms that are relevant to the teaching. He must be able to make statements about what the children know and do not know. Only if the teacher is provided with such information does he know whether he should continue to demonstrate a particular concept or move on to the next one. Since he must infer what children know from their performance, however, he must introduce tasks into the teaching demonstration. Demonstrations and tasks are therefore necessary components of any teaching activity.

The Distinction Between Teaching Routines and Tasks

A teaching routine is the demonstration that all instances of a concept can be treated in the same way. A routine consists of the specific ways a teacher treats all positive instances of a concept one way and all negative instances another way. The general assumption is that the children will apply the rule: the teacher treats them the same way; therefore they are the same in some respects. The routine also provides the child with a "model" of behavior that is to be used in tasks. It demonstrates how a signal or set of signals is used to refer to a concept. Later, when the child is tested, he will be expected to use the signal in the same way it had been demonstrated. He will be expected to "associate" the signal with the concept characteristics.

A *routine* consists of the ways that a teacher treats every concept instance in the same way. Perhaps all he does is show instances of the concept. His routine is described simply as "showing positive instances." Perhaps he shows both positive and negative instances and provides a differential signal for each type of instance. His routine is now described as "Showing positive instances and labelling them X; showing negative instances and labelling them Y." Perhaps he talks a great deal about each instance, but he always uses a par-

20

ticular word when referring to the concept. The routine is described accordingly.

A teaching routine is *not* a task.

It is possible for a teacher to "lecture" when demonstrating a concept. No response is required from the child. He is supposed to observe and somehow learn. Tasks always involve *responses*. Another difference is that a task is "discreet". It is a self-contained unit with a set of directions for responding and a particular set of responses that is acceptable. Not so with a routine. A routine usually consists of many different presentations. All are intended to function to induce further understanding of the concept, or stated differently, to provide further information about the set of characteristics that sets the concept instances apart from other instances. It is impossible to construct a routine that involves only a single presentation.

The *intent* of the teaching routine is different from that of the task. The routine is designed to *convey* information. The task is designed to test the information the child has received.

The Uniform Use of Signals

It is not enough to make the child aware of a concept; the routine must also teach him how to "code" the concept in such a way that he will be able to demonstrate that he has been taught the concept. If we simply show the child various instances of red, without providing any verbal signal, we *may* teach the concept of redness, but we will have no way of testing the child to determine whether or not he has been taught. We have failed to teach the behavior that is to be used in the tasks. Therefore, the child cannot be expected to perform adequately on a task in which we present objects and ask, "Is this red?" The word *red* has not been taught. A routine must do more than demonstrate the concept; it must also teach the *task conventions* that are associated with the concept. It must teach the signals that are to be used to test the child on his concept awareness.

A minimum teaching routine, therefore, involves a presentation of instances, usually positive instances and negative instances, and some kind of differential signal, one signal to tell the child when an instance is an instance of the concept and another to tell him when an instance is not a concept instance.

Note that the entire teaching procedure is based on the principles that:

(a) there are qualitative differences in things that can be "perceived" or observed in some way;

(b) by treating the positive instances in one way and by treating the negative instances in another way, we will

21

be able to demonstrate the qualitative difference we want to teach.

The child who is learning a concept does not know what that concept is. We present examples. He notes that we treat some of the examples in one way and some in another. The primitive learning in which he has previously engaged has taught him the principle that *if things are the same they can be treated in the same way and that if things are treated in the same way, they are the same in some respect.* When we treat one group of instances in the same way, we are giving him information. We are, in effect, saying "They're the same. All of these things share a set of characteristics. I cannot put into words what these characteristics are, but if you search, if you examine the objects, you will discover what the shared characteristics are. Those characteristics are the ones I refer to when I use the signal that I have introduced. The other signal describes examples that do not have the set of shared characteristics."

The process is purely one of "discovery". Our examples are the raw material from which the child must abstract the concept. Our signal is simply a general directive to let him know that we treat a group of instances in the same way. Why? Examine the instances and discover what they have in common. If we treat them the same, there must be a sameness in the instances.

Relationship Between Behavior and Concepts

We can resolve one of the questions that has been vigorously debated in psychology by referring to the basic assumption of any teaching demonstration: If things are treated in the same way, they do in fact share a unique set of characteristics. The question has to do with whether one should view concept learning in terms of "response associations" or in terms of "hypotheses." According to the present analysis, concept learning must be expressed in terms of hypotheses. The reason is that we can conclude that a child has learned a concept only if we interpret his behavior. Our interpretation must be based on behavior, but an interpretation is implied, especially when we deal with incorrect responses.

In the teaching situation, we operate according to the rule that if an instance has characteristic X, we use the signal Y. We expect the child to learn this rule. We expect him to *use* this rule. Only if he uses this rule will we be able to conclude that he has learned the concept. We infer his concept rule from his performance. When we view his performance we say in effect, "His behavior is an indication of his concept understanding." If he behaves as a person who has been taught the concept would behave, he has been taught the concept. If not, he has not been taught. The "hypotheses" interpretation of concept learning is introduced because it is necessary. The child must infer the rule from our presentation. We can only treat concept instances in the same way. He must infer from our behavior that there is something that *is* the same about the concept instances, and he must discover what the sameness is. Similarly, we must infer from his behavior—from the way he treats the various instances—what his rule is.

If a child treats couches and chairs in the same way, we conclude that his concept rule for chair is not sufficiently precise. We conclude that this rule is not consistent with the rule we are trying to teach. He has not been taught about the one-person-seating characteristics of chairs. We can now focus our teaching on the discrimination that he hasn't been taught. We "contradict" his rule. We do this by presenting things that are couches and presenting the signal that indicates they are not chairs. We create a contradiction by showing the child that his behavior is not consistent with ours. Therefore his rule is not the same as ours. He treats chairs and couches the same way. We say, "No. Look again. Revise your hypothesis."

Teaching routines are based on the assumption that neither the child nor the teacher has direct access to the other's concept awareness. Communications must be achieved through behavior. The teacher's behavior is his routine. The child's behavior is his response. Unless teacher and child assume that the other's behavior is "consistent" there can be no teaching and no corrections. When the teacher uses the same verbal signal to describe two things, the child must assume that there is a basis for treating the two things in the same way. Unless the teacher assumes that the child's behavior is consistent with a particular concept (regardless of the variety of errors the child makes) he cannot specify what type of correction is needed (or at least he cannot prescribe the most efficient remedy).

Usually a number of presentations is required either for the child to discover the relationship between the teacher's routine and the characteristics of the instances he presents and for the teacher to discover the relationship between the child's response pattern and the concept he is using. Both routines and responses are sequenced bits of information. Only when enough of the bits are pieced together can one receive information that is adequate for drawing a conclusion about the "rule" that is being used by the other.

Teaching One and Only One Concept

If a teacher presents a single instance of a concept, he cannot hope to teach that concept. This doesn't mean that some children won't learn the concept. It means simply that a child cannot be expected to learn from the presentation. If he learns, his performance will be a function both of past experience and chance. Let's say that a teacher holds up an apple and says, "This is a *glick*." Next, he holds up a red piece of cloth and says, "This is a *glick, too*." Is his demonstration adequate for teaching the concept *glick*? If it is, we should have enough information to say what *glick* is. However, we don't. *Glick* could be any of a number of concepts. The teacher could have been trying to tell the children, "This is an object," "This is in my hand", "This is red", "This is something that people use", and so forth.

Note that the teacher presented instances of the concept, and yet his demonstration was not capable of *teaching* the concept that he wanted to teach. This point is extremely important. There is a critical difference between constructing a routine that is merely consistent with a concept and constructing a routine that will teach that concept. The teacher who holds up an apple and says, "This is *red,*" is certainly providing the children with a true statement. He is certainly providing a demonstration that is consistent with the concept *red*. The apple is red. However, the routine is not adequate *because it is not consistent with one and only one concept*. His signal, "red", could refer to a host of concepts. An apple has many characteristics. It has a certain shape, a certain smell and color, and he is doing something with the apple. To which of these characteristics does *red* refer?

Viewed in another way, the teacher must present events and things to demonstrate concepts. However, the raw material that he uses is never consistent with only one concept. The physical thing we call "apple" is an instance of an infinite number of concepts. It is an instance of one, not two, not three . . . It is an instance of object, solid-object, solid-red object, hard object, hard-red object. The teacher must use instances, but he must use instances in such a way that his presentations is consistent only with the concept he wishes to teach. If he wants to teach the concept *person,* he may present the same concept instance that he introduced when he taught *John Baker,* when he taught *male,* when he taught *boy,* when he taught *running,* and so forth. He must now use this instance in such a way that the child is able to abstract the characteristics that comprise the concept *person*.

Constructing a Group of Concept Instances

If a particular concept, such as *person,* has a number of instances we can teach that concept only by creating a group of instances. The purpose of the group is simply to eliminate extraneous variables. When we present a single instance of *person* and signal that it is a positive instance, we are indicating that any of the characteristics of that object *may be* relevant to the concept. When we introduce another instance of the concept and identify it, we reduce the number of characteristics that are shared by the two instances. The first instance that we present may be a boy with freckles and red hair. The second instance may be a girl with no freckles and red hair. With the introduction of the second instance of person, we rule out the possibility that the designation *person* refers to the characteristics of boyness or freckleness. It may be a red-headed youngster, living thing, animal, etc. Our third instance of the concept may be a grey-haired old man. The shared characteristics of the group of positive instances is now reduced. Not all instances share the characteristic of being young or having red hair. By continuing to introduce instances, we can usually reduce the shared characteristics of the group to those that correspond to the shared characteristics that describe the concept.

However, we may induce a misrule unless we select examples with some care. What would happen if every instance of person we presented had red hair? The child might well learn the misrule that a *person* must have *red hair*. Note that the child's rule is perfectly consistent with our presentation. The shared characteristics of the group that we assembled included red hair. The misrule is therefore consistent with our group of positive instances. Our group was not consistent only with the concept we wanted to teach. It was also consistent with another concept—human with red hair.

To assemble a concept group that shares only the desired characteristics, the teacher must consult his knowledge of concept. What are the characteristics shared only by concept instances?

If a characteristic is not shared by all instances of a concept, it should not be shared by all members of the group of instances assembled to demonstrate the concept. The group of instances used to demonstrate the concept is actually a "sample" of the universe of positive instances. If the members of the sample share characteristics which are not shared by all members of the universe, it is a poor sample because it is not consistent with the concept the teacher wants to teach.

Not Instances

Even if the teacher provides a sample that has only those characteristics that are shared by all concept instances, the child may not learn the concept correctly. He may not learn the "scope" of the concept, which means simply that he may correctly identify all positive instances correctly, but he may indicate that some negative instances are positive instances. For example, if the teacher presents an adequate sample for the concept *person* without presenting any

25

not instances, he may later discover that the child thinks that all living things—including dogs, lions, and rose bushes—are persons. While his presentation was adequate for showing the characteristics that are shared by all persons, the presentation did not limit the characteristic to those shared *only by persons*. It is therefore possible for a child to construct a rule that is not limited.

If the child is expected to learn the limitations of the concept, the demonstration group must be limited. The kind of limitation that is adequate is determined by consulting the universe in which the concept was described. The various types of negative instances that are included in this universe must be represented in the group of instances used to demonstrate the concept. If couches and beds are included in the universe of the concept chair, couches and beds must be included in the sample presented to the child. According to the structure of the concept universe, one does not "have" the concept chair unless one can discriminate between chairs and not chairs (couches and beds in this case).

The Language Component of Teaching Routines

Language is used in a number of ways in a teaching routine. Basically, it functions as a signal that the teacher is treating the instances in the same way. When one is teaching concepts to relatively sophisticated children, language can be used as a substitute for a group of demonstration instances. Instead of presenting an actual group of things, the teacher can use a rule that describes the characteristics of the group. He can present the rule. "When you see the word *of* (e.g. one-half *of* 20 is 10) in a word problem it means *times*." Not only does this procedure reduce the memory load imposed on the child, it also provides for a less ambiguous presentation. The rule has less noise than the presentation of demonstration instances. It has no irrelevant features. The possibility of misunderstanding is therefore reduced. The child doesn't have to examine a number of word problems that can be translated into multiplication before discovering that the word *of* translates into *times*. He doesn't have to abstract this concept from the myriad irrelevant details in the various problems. He receives a verbal statement that concerns itself only with the critical aspects of the concept. It describes the entire class of positive instances.

Obviously, language has a potential economy, not only because it frees the teacher from the sometimes cumbersome presentation of instances, but also because it allows the teacher (and the child) to focus on the relevant characteristics of the positive instances more efficiently than one could normally hope to achieve with the presentation of instances. The verbal rule, if properly constructed, is a model of the concept.

Language is also useful in helping the child in his search for the characteristics that are shared by the concept instances. Language is not a substitute for an effective presentation of demonstration instances, but a language routine can greatly reduce the ambiguity rooted in a routine that does not make use of language. Let's say that a child has learned the concept *horse,* and we want to teach the child the concept brown. If we present a *horse* and call it brown, the child may assume that we are introducing another name for *horse.* To contradict this misrule without using language, we would have to proceed an instance at a time, showing the child that brownness is independent of horseness. If, however, we use statements we can alert the child to the independence with the presentation of the first instance.

"What is this? Yes, it's a horse. This horse is *brown.*" The function of the language component of the routine is to acknowledge that the horse is an instance of a concept the child has already learned. The statement about brown alerts the child to the fact that whatever brown is, it is not horse.

Another closely related advantage of language is that language conventions help the learner understand both what a concept is and what it is not. After a child has learned a number of words, he knows that a new word such as *glick* tells that the instances referred to as *glick* cannot also be referred to as *not-glick.* Similarly, a statement of fact, such as, "He sat on the floor," implies a great deal about what he did not do (and what *he* is not). Since verbal signals imply what characteristics instances of the concept have and what characteristics they do not have, a great economy is achieved through the use of language. When dealing with sophisticated children, the teacher often has to spend little time demonstrating not instances. Often children can do an amazing job of analyzing the meaning of a concept from a presentation of a few positive instances. They have learned that the new word is attempting to tell them about what the new concept is and what it is not.

A final advantage of language has to do with "cues." Language can be used to establish a more general function with respect to concepts that have a very specific function and may therefore be confused. Let's say that a child is having a great deal of trouble remembering the sound for the letter *h.* *He* confuses *h* with the letters *d* and *b.* Every time the teacher presents the letter *h,* she therefore introduces a special language routine. "This is that funny letter again . . ." She uses this routine only in connection with *h.* Through this routine, she is able to make *h* less similar than *d* and *b.* *H* becomes less similar because the teacher treats it in a different way than she treats any other letter. The "cue" that she provides helps to reduce confusion.

Coding concepts into language is an essential objective of a teaching program. Once a concept has been coded, it can be used in a variety of ways. It becomes a module that can be introduced to build a variety of complex conceptual structures.

Rules for Effective Routines

A concept implies the range of instances that must be presented, the *not* instances that must be presented, and the fact that some kinds of signals are used to distinguish between positive instances and not instances. However, there are any number of different ways that we can satisfy the teaching requirements implied by a concept. We could begin by teaching the child to respond appropriately to a particular instance (which is what is done in many traditional teaching situations). We could present concept instances that are irregularly spaced in time. We could use language-rich explanations in connection with our presentation of examples or minimum-language statements. Any routine will be adequate if it satisfies the teaching requirements implied by the concept, but obviously, not all routines that are adequate are equally desirable. Some are more efficient than others. There are two primary factors that provide direction for devising most efficient presentations:

(1) Human memory is limited. In dealing with young children and in many cases with sophisticated adults, one cannot assume that the learner will remember all of the instances that have been presented. In many cases, he will probably remember no more than the last two or three (unless the presentation of instances is designed to reduce the memory load). The problem of limited memory is magnified when instances of the concept are interspersed with extraneous examples. The casual presentation in which the child encounters an example of the concept every few days is bound to be less effective than a presentation in which the examples are massed together.

(2) Teaching a concept to a naive child involves less teaching than teaching the concept to a child who has been taught the concept incorrectly. A child who has learned to guess at words instead of reading them is more difficult to teach than a child who has not been taught how to read. Any presentation that is capable of generating misrules is less desirable than a presentation in which the misrules have been eliminated. To teach the concept *soft,* a teacher may give a young child a teddy bear. The teddy bear has a number of characteristics in addition to softness. It is capable of generating many potential misrules. A teacher who presents objects behind a child's back (so that he cannot see them) and who indicates after the child has touched an object whether or not it is *soft* is introducing fewer potential misrules.

Implications

The presentation with the least memory demand and the least misrule potential is the most desirable. Both the memory and the misrule potential can be determined by analyzing the presentation of concept instances.

A hint about how to construct effective presentational routines comes from the concept analysis. In the analysis we discussed "converting" positive instances into negative instances, and vice versa. If we were to introduce conversions into teaching demonstrations we would be able to demonstrate the specific functions and make the child aware of the critical differences between positive and negative instances. We would also reduce the memory load and reduce the "noise" in our presentation by holding many irrelevant characteristics of the presentation instances constant. For example, we could present an object that is *red*—perhaps a chair. After we indicate that it is red, it could change to another color, blue. "It's *not* red." It could again change into red. We could indicate, "It is red."

The presentation has ruled out all of the extraneous variables in the object except *one*— the color. Every detail of the object remains the same in both the positive and negative instances except color. Also, the memory load is reduced. We can change from red to not-red at a relatively rapid pace. The only aspect of the object that changes is the color, which means that the child can focus attention (and memory) on the critical variable.

By carrying the conversion idea a step further, we could devise a presentation that showed the child both something about the range of positive instances and about the limits of the concept. We present an object. That object continually changes shape, texture, position, and size. But it remains red. With every change, we indicate that it is red. After a few changes, the object changes from red to blue. We indicate that it is no longer red. It continues to change texture, shape, etc. but it remains blue. It changes back to red and we indicate that it is red. And so forth.

It would be possible to develop "ideal" concept-teaching sequences by using modern motion-picture and television techniques. However, the classroom and teacher and the program writer are not usually in a position to specify ideal presentations. They must usually settle for demonstrations that approach the deal.

The principles that they should follow in developing these are:

(1) Concentrate on the *specific* functions that the concept has with respect to other concepts. *Demonstrate* these functions by *converting*

positive instances into negative instances or vice versa. "Now the ball is not on the chair . . . Now the ball *is* on the chair." Nothing has changed but the position of the ball. In some cases, it is not possible to change an instance of a concept into a negative instance. The functional equivalence of changing it is to present an instance that is the same as the original in every respect except one. For example, two identical balls can be presented to the child. One is heavy and the other is not. The specific function of "heaviness" is demonstrated. The presentation works in the same way as if the same ball had been made first heavy and then light. All of the extraneous details in the presentation have been eliminated. This does not mean that the child would necessarily understand that objects other than balls can be called heavy. To demonstrate the scope of heaviness, one would have to present a range of objects that differ in such characteristics as size, shape, etc.

(2) Present the instances *quickly* so that the possibility of the child fixing on the appropriate set of characteristics is increased. The teacher should avoid what we might call "educamorphic" thought. Simply because he was not taught a concept in a particular manner does not mean that the manner is ineffective. A presentation will be effective if it satisfies the teaching requirements imposed by the concept and if it conforms relatively closely to an "ideal" presentation. It will be closer to the ideal if the instances are presented rather rapidly, with little or no interim activity to confuse the presentation. This point can be demonstrated nicely in beginning reading. Stop sounds are not introduced into the DISTAR reading program until children have mastered continuous sounds. Stop sounds are first introduced at the beginning of words in rhyming series.

The teacher has the children read the first three words. Then before presenting the stop-sound-first word, he summarizes, pointing to the first three words in turn. "Rat, mat, fat, so this must be ———". If the teacher goes too slowly when summarizing, the children will not produce the correct response. They will not see what the common characteristics of the words *rat, mat,* and *fat* are. By summarizing more rapidly, the teacher can almost always prompt the correct response.

30

CHAPTER IV

TASKS AND TASK ANALYSIS

In Chapter 1, we referred to the general tests that are implied by a concept and its functions with respect to other concepts. This chapter deals with the relationship between the tests that are implied by analysis of a concept and the actual tasks that are created. When we translate tests of concept understanding into tasks, we move from possible behavior to specific behavior, from a range of possible ways to test understanding of a concept to specific ways. Concept analysis yields testing specification (what the task or set of tasks should test). Theoretically, we would accept any test that tested the characteristics of the concept disclosed by our analysis. The concept analysis assumes that there will be some kind of performance and some kind of signal to perform, but neither the signal nor the performance is specified.

We cannot test without introducing specific tasks; yet two tasks that test the same "understanding" may be quite different. Both of the following tasks test a child's ability to discriminate between chairs and couches:

(1) Present pictures of chairs and couches. Before presenting pictures, instruct child: "Touch every picture of a chair. If it's a chair, touch it." Correct response: touching chairs.

(2) Present pictures of chairs and couches. Before presenting pictures, instruct child: "Indicate which of the pictures that I am going to present is a chair by writing the word *chair* on your paper every time I present a chair. If I present a picture of something other than a chair, write the name of illustrated object on your paper." Correct response: child writes appropriate names.

Clearly, one of these tasks is more difficult than the other. Stated differently, the number of possible reasons for failing one of the tasks is greater than the number of possible reasons for failing the other. The child may fail the second task simply because he doesn't know how to write, or because he doesn't understand some of the critical words presented in the instructions. The response required is more complicated, and the signal to respond is more complicated. The fact that two such discrepant tasks can be used to "test" the same discrimination points up a serious problem in any analysis of tasks and problem-solving techniques. A program that is designed to teach the child to pass the second task would have to engage in far more teaching than a program designed to teach the child to pass the first task. We can look at the problem in another way. Let's say that a child has been taught the chair-couch discrimination and that he can pass the first task (and similar tasks) but not the second. Has he actually been taught the discrimination or hasn't he? If we say that he has, we are opening the door to a number of problems. For example, in a different situation, a child may demonstrate that he can form four groups of objects, each group containing three objects. He may be able to tell us that he has a total of twelve objects. However, he fails this task: "How many would you end up with if you counted by three four times?" and this task: "What's four times three? Figure it out." Are we satisfied that the child has been taught how to multiply?

Unless we specify our tests in terms of specific tasks, we do not know precisely what the child has been taught. We don't know the signals or the routines that have been taught. However, some tasks designed to test a particular discrimination seem "fair" or reasonable, while others seem unfair. An analysis of tasks should provide some kind of guidelines for constructiing tasks that test what they are designed to test and do so in a way that is fair.

What Is a Task?

"The ball on the table" is not a task. "Put the ball on the table" and "Is the ball on the table?" are. They contain a signal to respond. The signal to respond is an essential feature of a task. From an analytical standpoint, this feature presents problems. It is impossible to test a child's understanding of a concept in an unambiguous way of using a task. If we were to construct a task that tested only his concept understanding, that task could be failed for only one reason—lack of sufficient concept understanding. However, the structure of a task implies that the child can fail a task simply because he has not been taught the convention for responding. In other words, he may know the concept, but be unable to demon-

32

strate his knowledge. If we ask, "Is this a ball?" he may not respond, or he may take the ball and put it on the table. Yet, it is theoretically possible that he understands the concept *ball*.

In order to perform adequately on a particular task, the child must learn not only the concept that is being tested but also the specific response rules that are introduced in the task. Unless he learns both the concept and the conventions for responding, he will not pass the task. When the teacher asks, "What color is this?" he must know that the task calls for a particular type of operation, namely judging the color of the object. He must have been taught the word that stands for the concept *red*. And he must know that the task calls for him to use either the word red or some other color word. Note that the task implies a specific type of investigation and response. Investigate the *color* of the object. Respond with the appropriate *color name*.

Obviously, this test goes far beyond a test of the child's concept understanding. Tests of other concepts are embedded in the task. We call these *task-related concepts*. They don't derive from the concept that is being tested. They derive from the need to observe the child's concept knowledge as behavior. The basic task-related concept is—respond to the signal that calls for a response. Each task, however, presents a far more specific instance of this rule. The task "What color is this?" calls for a very specific type of investigation and a very specific class of responses. The child may answer by saying *blue* (in response to a red object), which would be an incorrect response but one that is quite consistent with the response conventions of the task. If the child responds by saying, "yes", however, he has not been taught the response conventions that apply to any task of the form, "What color is ....," or perhaps "What is this?"

That a task-related concept is actually a concept can be demonstrated quite easily. Let's say that when we snap our fingers the child is to indicate the color of the object we present. Both the task in which we ask, "What color is this?" and the finger snapping task share an important characteristic. They both call for precisely the same operation and response. They differ in many obvious respects. The "syntax" of the finger snapping task differs radically from that of the color question. *For any given task we could construct an indefinite number of tasks that have the same operational characteristics.*

Tasks can also be grouped according to their sensory-input charasteristics. The task, 'Give me the car," is similar to the task, "Give me the card." Yet, the operation that is called for by each task is quite different. These tasks have a specific function with respect to each other in terms of their sensory-input characteristics. We can convert the task, "Give me the car" into "Give me the card" by adding a single sound to the original string of sounds. The tasks "Give me the car" and "Hand me that toy vehicle" have a general function with respect to each other so far as sensory-input characteristics are concerned, but they have the same operational characteristics. To convert "Give me the car" into "Hand me that toy vehicle" would involve extensive changes. Yet, the operation would remain intact.

The analysis of tasks is indeed complex, primarily because tasks can be viewed both operationally and in terms of their sensory-input characteristics. The distinction between the different types of specific functions is important to the programmer, however, because he is responsible for systematic teaching. He must be aware of the possible sources of task confusion. If he programs tasks that have similar sensory-input characteristics, he must be prepared to provide cues to help the children discriminate the signals. (He must create a more general function by treating the two instances differently). If he is to program the letters *b* and *d*, he must anticipate the child's possible confusion (since *b* can be converted into *d* by flipping it). He must be particularly wary about programming tasks in which two tasks have a specific function with respect to each other both in terms of sensory-input characteristics and operational characteristics. The task, "Touch your shoe" has a specific operational function with respect to the task "Touch your shoes". The only difference is the number of specified objects in the group. Also, "Touch your shoe" has a specific sensory-input function with respect to "Touch your shoes". We can convert the first task into the second simply by adding a sound to the last word. The potential confusion for this task pair is relatively great because the discriminations that the child must learn are relatively fine. The difference between the operations called for is very specific, and the differences of sensory-input is very specific.

The types of specific functions a task has with respect to other tasks tells the programmer the types of discriminations the child must learn to make. Must he learn to hear sound discriminations? Must he learn to discriminate between two operations that are similar? The programmer can arrive at an answer to these questions by consulting the tasks that are to be introduced. Note that reference is made to tasks, not to a single *task*. Tasks never occur in isolation. Consequently, they must not be taught as if they occur in isolation. If a teacher teaches a child to pick up a ball in response to the command "Pick up a ball", the teacher may have taught the child the concept or may not have. After training, the child may pick up a ball when someone says "Tie your shoe", "Hand me an apple", or

34

"Is your name, Jerry?" The response is overgeneralized, and the overgeneralization is a function of instruction. The child had not been taught that the response of picking up a ball is appropriate only for "pick up a ball", or commands that have the same operational characteristic. The child has not actually learned the command unless he is able to demonstrate that he can discriminate between this task and other tasks that have a relatively specific function with respect to the initial task.

Constructing Task Classes

We can construct a class of tasks in much the same way we construct a universe for a concept. The procedure is as arbitrary. The positive instances of the task class are the tasks that have the same operational characteristics. (Give me the ball. Give the ball to me. Hand me the ball. Hand the ball to me. Will you please give me the ball, etc.). The negative instances are tasks that have different operational characteristics than the positive instances. (Throw the ball to me. Tie your shoe. Stand up. etc.). As noted above, a positive instance of the task may have a specific operational function with respect to a negative instance; a positive instance may have a specific sensory-input function with respect to a negative instance. Or a positive instance may have both a specific operational function and a specific sensory-input function with respect to a negative instance.

We can construct the task class so that there is only one negative instance in the class and this negative instance has a general function with respect to the positive instance. Or we can construct the universe so that there are many negative instances, some of which have specific functions with respect to the positive instance. The universe that we construct tells us the kind of discrimination that the child must learn to make if he is to avoid confusing any tasks selected from the task class.

Task Forms

If we are given the task, "Put the ball in the box", we construct a "task form" that applies not only to this task, but to a range of similar tasks. *This form should allow for demonstrating all of the specific functions of the task,* all of the discriminations the child must learn. (put, throw, etc.), (ball, cup, bowl), (in, at, over), (pan, desk, box). From this form a number of tasks can be created:

Put the cup in the box.

Throw the ball at the desk.

Put the cup in the pan.

The universe is not constructed through a process of random selection. The words must be selected in such a way that no nonsense instructions result. Once a task class has been constructed the class constitutes the test of a child's task understanding. We do not say that he has been taught "Put the ball on the pan" until he can demonstrate that he can perform consistently on all tasks in the class. *To test the understanding of a task is actually to test understanding of the class.* While this stipulation may seem harsh on first encounter, it is necessary. We have no way of knowing that the child can actually discriminate between the original task and others with which it is likely to be confused unless the child is able to demonstrate that he can handle all tasks in the class.

More Traditional Analysis

A similar type of task class may result from more traditional forms of task analysis, but the similarity is not guaranteed. We can examine a task and ask ourselves, "What must the child learn before he can handle this task?" We will note certain components—responses to signals in the task and concept words. However, through an analysis of this type, the range of discriminations that the child must be able to make is not clearly articulated. One task analyst may intuitively know that the child cannot handle the task unless he can demonstrate an ability to discriminate between the tasks and other "similar" tasks, but a second analyst may not know this. The second analyst may attempt to analyze a task in which the child is given six beads and a box and is told to "Put all of the beads in the box." The analyst may ask himself, "What must the child learn before he can handle this task?" The answer, he may conclude, is that he must learn to put all six beads in the box when he is told to do so. The teaching that is implied is to present the signal and then to follow it with a demonstration of the response. While this type of teaching may be adequate for some children in some teaching situations, it is not always adequate. The analyst may break the operation down, teaching the child first to put beads in the box in response to the signal, "Box." Later the analyst may introduce the signal, "In the box." And many steps later, "Put all of the beads in the box." The child has been taught all he needs to know to handle that task, if that task were the only one the child would ever encounter. The program (and the analysis) is poor, however, if the child will ever encounter similar tasks.

Task analysis is not a substitute for concept analysis, nor does it supersede concept analysis. Task analysis is useful only in giving the programmer a "fix" on the types of operations that must be taught and the type of confusion that may result with the introduction of a particular task taken from a particular universe of tasks.

The Meaning of Task Signals

A task, in one sense, is an irreducible unit. It is more than the sum of its parts. A task is a signal to perform in a certain way. Within a task, however, are other signals—words. The assumption is that when a given word is put in the task it has a meaning. Ideally, it has the same meaning as it does in other tasks. If its meaning were to change from task to task, there wouldn't be much point in having tasks because they could scarcely function as a signal for instances that share a particular set of characteristics. Let's say that there was a word, the meaning of which varied randomly from task to task. The task would be as informative as this one, "Put the .... on the table." The child cannot respond consistently because he has no way of knowing what characteristics are represented by ....

Task learning is based on the assumption that if the teacher treats two things the same way, they have the same set of characteristics. If he calls two objects "chair" those two objects share certain characteristics. Task learning is premised on the assumption that the words used within the task are always treated in the same way. What this means is that if the teacher knows that he will present the word red in a task, he must teach the meaning of red as it is to be used in the task. He must show the children instances of red. All of these instances have the same set of characteristics, and he will use the signal to treat them the same.

Reducing a Concept

Teaching the meaning of words is an important derivation of task analysis. However, this teaching can become extremely confused unless one adheres to the principle that the programmer has a great deal of latitude in "constructing" concepts. He can, for the sake of more efficient instruction, construct concepts that are more narrowly defined than the concept is generally conceived by adults. Or, he can construct concepts that extend beyond the arbitrary limits established by adult convention.

This does not mean that the programmer has license to be irresponsible. Ultimately, he is responsible for teaching the concepts as they are generally understood. He is not required to teach full-blown concepts immediately, however. Nor is he initially required to teach all of the concepts that are implied by a word that he introduces. Almost any concept word that can be introduced has many meanings. When a person says, "I see red," he is using the word *red* in a different way than he would when he says. "I see red clouds." The three limitations placed on the programmer are these:

(1) If he reduces a concept to a more simplified form, he must teach the "main idea" of the concept;

(2) If he reduces a concept, he must introduce at least one group of *not* instances into the universe of instances;

(3) If he expands a concept beyond its conventional boundaries, he must subdivide the universe so that the conventional concept can also be taught.

These limitations can be summarized by saying that the programmer must make sure that he is not constructing a monster which cannot be *modified through additions or subtractions* to conform to the conventional concepts. He has to program the key characteristics so that he has a solid foundation upon which to build.

In order to reduce a pre-established concept that is signalled by a word, the programmer must first understand the concept as it is used in everyday adult life. He should not, however, become too concerned with the "gray" area of concepts, nor should he consult a dictionary. He should either consult his own experience or the experience of the person who is familiar with the concept. He should try to distill from the examination of the concept the *key* characteristics, that is, the characteristics that cover most of the instances. If possible, he may find characteristics that cover all of the instances. He should recognize, however, that almost every concept has a gray area. For example, the concept of *living* (as in living thing) has a gray area. The concepts human being, plant, animal—all have gray areas.

A gray area consists of relatively few instances that can be included in the concept class only if a more detailed set of characteristics is used to describe the concept instances. The question raised by the gray area is one of diminishing returns. Is the inclusion of a few additional instances worth the effort of discrimination programming that is implied? This question can often be answered negatively by applying the principle that the learner has limited memory. If the concept *living* can be programmed using a single criterion, it is initially more "teachable" than an expanded set of criteria.

The reduction is allowable, however, only if it can be demonstrated that *by the addition of criteria* it will conform relatively closely to the conventional concept. The programmer should not be held responsible for precise conformity because many of the concepts that we use are not precise in the gray area. The programmer should therefore be allowed the benefit of the doubt on fine points.

Note, however, that the continuity between the reduced concept and the more conventional concept must be expressed simply in terms of additional criteria, not changes in criteria. This principle applies even when one moves from everyday language concepts to technical concepts. The everyday concept of *red* is quite different from the physicist's concept. Yet, if the everyday concept is properly programmed, the physicist's concept can be expressed by adding criteria. Similarly, the concept of metal can be expressed through addition if metal is initially taught properly.

We can illustrate the procedure of adding conventions by referring to the concept *long*. For the initial presentation, the programmer may decide to treat *long* simply as polar, eliminating the possibility that things can be longer or longest. However, he must develop programming steps that allow him to make a transition from the concept that he initially creates to a non-polar version of long, merely by adding to what he has already programmed.

Initially, he introduces tasks in which the child is presented with a variety of object pairs. One object is longer than the other. The absolute length of the objects varies from pair to pair. First, the objects are identified either as long or not long. Later, the not long instances are introduced as short. "Is this snake long? . . . That's right, this snake is not long. This snake is short." Finally, the children are tested on their ability to identify various objects (presented in pairs) as either long or short. When the children pass this test, they have demonstrated that they have mastered the concept taught.

Now, the programmer makes a transition, using what he has already programmed. He presents a series of objects that are arranged in order of increasing size. He points to two of the objects, and tells the children "One of these lines is long. Which one? . . . Yes, this line is *longer* . . . Is this other line longer? . . . No, this other line is shorter." The demonstration is repeated, selecting different pairs of lines from the series. After the children are able to describe pairs of lines using the terminology, "This line is longer," the programmer includes another step. "You say this line is longer? Longer than which line? . . . Yes, longer than that line . . . This line is longer than that line." The programmer then introduces construction tasks in which the children are arranging sticks in order of increasing or decreasing size. "Here's a stick . . . You put down a stick that is longer . . . Okay, now look at this stick you put down. Put down another stick that is longer"

Longest is introduced in connection with a series arranged in order of increasing size. "Find the stick that is not shorter . . . This stick is not shorter. It is not shorter than this stick . . . It is not shorter than this stick . . . It is *longest*."

The transition from the programmer's initial concept to the more conventional concept was achieved through simple additions. At every step, the demonstrations began with what had already been programmed. The programmer's initial concept was therefore justified.

Longer and longest are demonstrated to be special cases, but cases that are perfectly continuous with the procedures programmed for handling long. No basic changes in the initial concept were introduced, simply additions that apply to "exceptional" cases.

Constructing Tasks That Are Fair

It is not possible to construct tasks that can be failed for just one reason. Does it follow, therefore, that tasks that can be failed for numerous reasons are inferior to tasks that can be failed for only a few reasons? No. The task, "Discuss the political implications of Darwin's theory of evolution, especially as it relates to Western Europe," may be fair. The task, "Circle all objects that are either found in the house or in the yard" may be fair. The task, "Say what I say: *red,*" may be fair. Tasks demonstrate what has been taught. If the children have been taught the skills that are necessary to handle a particular type of task, they should be tested on what they have been taught. If they have been taught about the impact of Darwin on the Western European political scene, they should be tested on this. If they have been taught to respond to such commands as "Say what I say: ...." They should be tested on this.

The problem with more complicated tasks lies in the area of educational diagnosis. If a child passes a complex task, we can affirm, "Yes he can handle this task. He has been taught the component skills." If he fails the task, however, we are often at a loss to specify what we should have to teach him in order to assure passing performance.

The tasks noted above are fair if they are paired with other tasks that tell something about the child's ability to handle the component concepts presented in the task. The purpose of the component tasks is to show why a child failed the item, if he fails it. We could present the task, "Put all of the beads in the box" to two children, one a three-year old and the other a nine-month old. Both may fail the task, but the three-year old won't fail it in the same way as the nine-month old. The latter may look at us and smile before picking up the box and banging it several times on the floor. The three-year old may put most but not all of the beads into the box. The program implied for the three-year old would not be the same as that for the infant. To specify a program, we must have detailed information, which means that tasks must be designed to yield the information we need.

The problem of fair tasks is most critical when one is working with children who are learning basic task operations and motor responses. "Draw a circle on the paper" may be failed because the child, al-

40

though he has an adequate understanding of circle, cannot draw a circle. This test is fair if the investigator is testing the child's ability to draw a circle. If the investigator is trying to test the child's understanding of circle, however, the test is not fair. It is similar to a test in which you are required to demonstrate your knowledge of great Americans by drawing their pictures. Obviously, you could provide other types of demonstrations that you can recognize George Washington and do not confuse him with other great Americans; however, you may fail the task. Similarly, an investigator may test a child's ability to produce the sound *rrr,* and the child may fail. "Say what I say: *run.*" Response; "wun". The investigator may begin response training at this point; however, he will achieve an economy if he first presents a series of tests like these: "Look at the picture, and tell me if I say it right. Listen: rabbit. Did I say it right? . . . Wabbit. Did I say it right? . . . The boy is wunning. Did I say it right? . . . The boy is running. Did I say it right?" It may be that the child needs some training in discriminating between the sensory-input characteristics of *r* and *w* sounds. It may be that the child can move into speech production exercises.

The Use of Generalized Operations

One way of constructing basic tests so that they can be failed primarily for only one reason is to use generalized operations. Responding to yes-no questions involves a generalized operation. The same response conventions, the same set of responses, and the same type of investigation is called for by any yes-no question. By pairing a series of these questions with *what* questions (the answer to which varies as the presentation of objects or events varies) the teacher can get a relatively good fix on the child's understanding of the concept and his ability to code his understanding into appropriate language. "Is this a ball? . . . Is this a man? . . . Is this a tree? . . . What is this? . . . Yes, it's a ball."

Another generalized response is selecting the concept instances from a larger display. The rules that apply to one selection task apply to all. This is not to say that these tasks are "non-verbal". They have a very obvious verbal component. Unless the child understands what concept and what kind of operation is represented by the teacher's signal when she says, "Find the ball," the child *cannot* consistently pass the test. The task is far from being pure, but it is closer to a realistic test of concept understanding than one in which the child is required to produce a complex response.

Criterion Referenced Testing

Traditionally, the objective of a test is to tell something about the child, usually about his natural aptitude. The intent of traditional testing is not to give us unambiguous information about what the child has been taught. The teacher, by virtue of his role, cannot be concerned with aptitude. Aptitude does not translate into what the teacher should do to teach the child something. A child's "aptitude" must therefore be rephrased and expressed in terms of what the child knows and doesn't know. The more specific the statements about his knowledge, the less the possibility that the teacher will teach the child something that is unimportant. If the teacher assumes that a child fails a task because he doesn't know the skill that the task is designed to test, she may provide a remedy that is not needed. Diagnostic tests of the child's understanding are extremely important. We refer to tests that allow for relatively precise statements about the child's knowledge as *criterion-referenced tests.*

The only type of acceptable task, from the standpoint of teaching, is the criterion-referenced task, simply because it translates into the language of the teacher. It specifies what kind of environmental manipulation is implied if the child is to meet the desired criterion of performance. Criterion-referenced tasks are required in the teaching sequence as well as the formal testing situation. The teacher paces the presentation according to how the children perform on the various tasks that are presented. If tasks are presented frequently, the teacher is able to maintain a relatively accurate record of what the children know. This record allows the teacher to proceed at maximum speed, which means spending the time that is required to teach a particular skill and then proceeding to the next skill without delay. The economy of this approach is achieved in terms of:

(a) more precise corrections of mistakes;

(b) less time devoted to skills which are irrelevant or tangential to the desired criterion of performance;

(c) less time devoted to unnecessary performance on skills that have been taught (but that will be used in higher-order tasks);

(d) a more concise curricular sequence.

Concluding Remarks

The structure of tasks implies a unique form of learning. A child may learn through experience with matches, stoves, and open fires that fire has a set of characteristics. All instances of fire, he learns, share a set of characteristics, and they are all to be treated in the same way. Physical contact with all instances should be avoided. After the child has learned about both the shared characteristics and the rule for treating instances in the same way, the child may be introduced to the signal, *fire.* The signal is an extension of the rule that the child has learned. You treat them all the same way in one respect (avoiding physical contact); therefore, you can treat them in the same way in another respect (identifying all instances with the same label). This type of learning is non-task learning.

In task learning, the child is given a signal and is asked to (a) discover which characteristics all of the instances share, and (b) express his awareness by following the operation specified in the task. Hopefully, the initial tasks involve generalized operations. "Is this line long? . . . Is this line long, now? . . ." The teacher treats all instances of long in the same way. *The child must discover why.* What are the characteristics that are shared only by the positive instances? Find the rule. The process is one of discovery. The teacher can simplify the process of discovery by reducing the noise in the presentation. He can present a sufficient number of examples. The child, however, must respond to the task. Unless he performs, the teacher receives no information. For this reason, the task can be viewed as a basic instructional component, an essential ingredient of a teaching presentation. The teacher tests and demonstrates, tests and demonstrates—always gearing the demonstration to the children's task performance. Tasks and the other basic instructional component, the teaching routine, are thereby wed together to form an effective teaching sequence.

CHAPTER V

PROGRAMMING

Programming is the sequencing of tasks and teaching demonstrations so that the children learn more thoroughly and more rapidly. Unless children are able to learn more thoroughly and more rapidly than they would in a traditional program, the material is not actually programmed.

The test of programmed material is this: At any given point in a program, a child may make a variety of mistakes. The teacher has to correct these mistakes. If she can correct them by using demonstrations that have already been presented in the program, the material is programmed. If she has to introduce a new explanation, the material is not programmed. If the correction procedure is effective, it should have been included earlier in the program to buttress against the mistake before it is made. Preventing mistakes is usually more efficient than correcting them after they have been made.

Viewed in another way, programming is the sequencing of educational objectives so that the teacher always knows precisely what to teach the child. If the teacher knows exactly why the child has failed a task, she knows exactly what to teach him. Programming enables her to make more definitive statements about what to teach because material that is programmed teaches only one content skill at a time. If a child fails a task, the teacher is reasonably sure that he has mastered all the component skills except for one. She is probably able to diagnose his learning problem more accurately and prescribe a remedy that will be both appropriate and economical.

Task Programming

The most rudimentary type of programming is what we might call task programming. We start with a task, and we analyze the words and operations that are involved in the task. We set up a series of teaching routines and tasks for each of the component skills. If the tasks that we present to teach a component skill involve new words or operations, we break these tasks down. We continue in this manner until we have broken the program down to a point where a rat could start on it.

Most educational programming involves an approach that is far more sophisticated than task programming. Although a task program may teach children the skills that are involved in the complex task from which the program is generated, there is no reason to believe that the program will be particularly efficient. It may be adequate, but it may also be highly redundant, slow, and may teach the children behaviors that work well on the task to be mastered, but that have no potential in setting the stage for other tasks that are to be presented later in the program.

Task programming begins with the assumption that tasks are given. This is not the case. The program developer has a great deal of latitude in selecting the tasks that he will use as the basis for his programming. He must design tasks, and he must design them in such a way that they teach the concepts he wishes to teach. In most cases, his routines will have multiple roles, teaching specific concepts and setting the stage for future concepts. Unless the program begins with an analysis of the concepts, not with tasks, the program will probably be only modestly efficient and therefore be capable of demonstrating only slight performance advantages over routines that are not "programmed".

Efficient Programming

The secret to efficient programming lies in the structure of concepts. Let's say that we assemble a random group of instances. The chances are that we will be able to *order* these instances. We might note that each of the subgroups A, B, and C have unique characteristics. However, all instances in subgroups A, B, C share a set of characteristics. All are the same in some respect. These concepts (A, B, C, and the broader concept) form a *cluster*. If we wanted to teach somebody the structure of this cluster, we would first have to teach him to identify members of each of the subgroups. And we would have to demonstrate that all instances are the same in some respect. We would have to teach on two different levels, first the level of the individual concepts, then on the level of the broader concept. There are different ways we could go about devising such instruction. If we follow task-programming procedures, we would teach each level, a fine-grained step at a time. A more efficient approach, however, is to teach on both levels at the same time, by setting up routines so that (a) the different subconcepts would be clearly demonstrated, and (b) there would be a demonstration that every instance in every subgroup could be treated the same way in some respect. That every instance can be treated in the same way demonstrates that every instance is the same in some respect. That the instances within a given subgroup are treated differently from instances in the other subgroups demonstrates that there are three individual concepts within the broader concept.

While the foregoing discussion may seem somewhat abstruse, it outlines the strategy that leads to efficient programming. Perhaps the introduction of a specific application will clarify the approach.

The concept *soft* is quite different from the concept *wet*. Yet, both are instances of the same broader concept. They are both instances of the broader concept we call polars or opposites. All opposites share a set of unique characteristics. If something is not wet, we have another word that describes that object—dry. If something is not soft, we have a word that describes that object—hard. Both *soft* and *wet* share a set of characteristics. If we want the child to learn that they share the set of characteristics, we must treat them as instances of the same concept, which means that he must treat them in the same way. This doesn't mean that he can call all wet things soft or all soft things wet. *We must treat wet and soft as apparently independent concepts. At the same time, we must introduce some kind of routine that allows us to treat both wet and soft as instances of the same concept.*

We can achieve both the immediate educational objective of teaching *wet* and *soft* and the secondary objective of teaching something about the structure of polars by introducing a set of tasks as a part of the routine for teaching all polars.

When teaching wet, we introduce the task, "I'm thinking of something and it is not wet. What do you know about it?"

When teaching soft, we introduce the task, "I'm thinking of something that is not soft, what do you know about it?"

Polars have a specific function with respect to non-polars. In a polar group, there are only two entities (hard-soft, dry-wet, little-big, etc.). In a non-polar group, there are more than two entities. (The group of words that describe the position of an object—in or under,

47

etc.—comprise a nonpolar group). We can convert a polar group to a non-polar group simply by adding a third member. This implies a discrimination that must be programmed. Additional exercises can be introduced to demonstrate the difference between polars and non-polars. "I'm thinking of something that is not damp. What do you know about it?"

The routine in the preceding example is designed to teach concept clusters. These routines must have certain properties if they are to succeed:

(1) They must be constructed according to a knowledge of the structure of what is to come, not in terms of tasks, but in terms of the concepts which are to be programmed.

(2) They must be constructed so that characteristics which are not perceptively obvious can be demonstrated; in other words, they must show rather clearly how all of the instances in the cluster are the same. We can't see how soft is the same as wet. They are the same because they share certain logical properties.

(3) They must provide for a compelling demonstration that all instances within the broader concept are the same. It is not enough to tell the children that soft and wet are opposites (but not of each other). The routine must demonstrate what this means.

Concept Clusters

There are a number of concepts that imply some kind of sensory investigation. One doesn't know whether or not an object is red unless he looks at it. Similarly, one doesn't know whether an object is in a particular position, is a particular kind of object, or has certain sensory characteristics unless one conducts a sensory investigation. Note that color, position, size, shape, etc., reside in objects. We cannot talk about position without assuming an object. We cannot talk about color without assuming an object. This means that it is impossible to teach concepts such as color and shape without introducing objects. Yet, we must be able to demonstrate that we are referring not to the object but to some characteristic of the object.

When we teach these concepts, we must show, through the use of a similar routine that the same type of investigation is involved in handling each concept, and that the concepts share the characteristic of "residing in " objects.

By beginning with the broader concept (the characteristics shared by color, prepositions, etc.) *we are able to place stipulations on the routines that we use to teach every one of the individual concepts*

48

that share the characteristics noted above. In other words, we know that the teaching routine for presenting *big* should have elements that are the same as the routine for teaching *red*. Furthermore, since we know *how* these concepts are the same, we are able to stipulate what the routine must do—treat the residual characteristic of each concept in the same way and demonstrate that sensory investigation is implied.

On the level of the individual concept, we must provide a demonstration that is adequate to teach the concept, with emphasis on the specific functions it has with respect to other concepts in the universe. When we put the requirements that derive from the broader concept with the requirements imposed by the individual concepts, we have a set procedure *for teaching individual concepts*. First we identify the concept; then we present a statement that describes the concept we are teaching.

This is a toy. This toy is *big*. Look at it.

Later, we introduce a task in which we demonstrate the function of the empirical investigation.

I'm going to show you a toy? Is that toy big? . . . You don't know until I show it to you.

While this example may seem trivial in some respects, it illustrates the basic procedure that should be used to sequence a series of educational objectives. It also illustrates the problem of programming "generalizations" and the problem of using efficient language.

Generalizations

From the standpoint of programming there is no such thing as generalization. If we were interested in measuring individual differences in children, generalization would be an acceptable construct. We would provide a demonstration of the concept using a limited sample of instances, all of which have characteristics that are not shared by other instances of the concept. We would then test the children on a range of instances that differ in various respects from those in the original set. Different children will perform differently. However, the generalization was not taught. The original demonstration was inadequate because it concentrated only on a segment of the instances that share the concept characteristics, not on a broad sample of instances.

From the standpoint of programming, there are only concepts, not generalizations. This point was made earlier, but it deserves repetition because it is critically important to programming. If a programmer expects the children to respond to instances of a concept in the same way, he must show them, through appropriate sampling and appropriate task construction, that all of these instances can be treated in the same way and therefore share a set of characteristics. This principle applies to task-related concepts as well as content concepts.

Analyzing Efficiency of Routines

There are two levels of efficiency for a given teaching routine. On the first level, we are concerned with an individual concept. Are the components of the routine—the statements, examples and tasks— smooth? Do they teach the essential characteristics of the concept without introducing a great deal of presentational noise? On the second level, we are concerned with the relationship between the routine for the individual concept with routines for other concepts that share the same set of characteristics. Is the routine designed so that all instances of the broader concept can be fitted into a variation of the routine?

Any teaching routine must be evaluated on both the first and second level of efficiency. *But the second-level considerations must be given priorities over the first.* A routine may have near maximum efficiency over the range of individual and broader concepts, although it may be possible to look at the routine as it is used to teach any particular concept and say, "I can simplify that procedure," or "I can think of a faster way to teach that." There may be faster ways, but the general assumption is that the routine that programs the cluster in connection with each instance of the individual concepts will achieve a great savings over a series of different routines designed to achieve the same educational objectives. There is less new learning involved in the general routine. This savings in new learning should show up as the child proceeds through the program. He should be able to handle new instances of the routine with increasing speed. He follows the same procedures and he responds to a similar set of cues. Furthermore, an economy is achieved by teaching the generalized procedure at the same time the individual concepts are being taught.

Let's say that a teacher wants to teach a cluster of four concepts. If she introduces a different routine for each concept, she must actually use *five* routines to achieve the same learning as one could achieve using one basic routine with four variations. The reason is that the single routine teaches the desired "generalization". The teacher who uses different routines to program the desired generalization must introduce another routine after she has taught the individual concepts. This routine demonstrates that all four concepts are instances of the same concept. This routine would bear a striking resemblance to the routine used in the more efficient presentation. It would have to demonstrate that all of the instances can be treated in the same way.

Note that an efficient routine teaches two concepts at the same time. But these concepts are never on the same level. To try to teach red and big at the same time would invite chaos, simply because it would be very difficult to control the presentational variables in such a way that the child would be able to isolate the specific functions that describe each concept. However, the second-level or broader concept does not interfere with the individual concepts, simply because instances of the individual concepts are also instances of the broader concept.

The Sacrificial Instance

In cluster programming, the instances of the broader concept are presented only through the individual concepts that are being taught. Conversely, *when a child learns the first individual concept, he learns the general operation or procedure for handling all instances of the broader concept.* When he learns the first concept, he must learn not only the specific concept but the structure of the broader concept. For example, when he learns his first polar (assuming that the routine is adequate) he learns a form of the rules needed to handle all polars.

The problem associated with this double-learning requirement of the first instance can be observed by a toddler who is learning to answer why questions. The toddler's mother reads a story to the child. In this story a why question is presented. "Why was Charley sleepy?" The correct answer: "Because he stayed up late and watched TV." But the child answers the questions inappropriately. The mother presents the question and gives the correct answer. She then goes on with the story. The teaching procedure is repeated for days, after which the toddler is able to answer the question. However, the child now answers all why questions by saying, "He stay and watch TV." The mother teaches the child to respond correctly to a second why question, and a third. Suddenly, the child is able to answer a variety of why questions, including those that he has never encountered before.

The child was required to learn a system for answering why questions. To learn the system however, he had to be exposed to enough instances of why questions to see what all had in common. (Their common characteristic was not that all are answered with, "He stay and watch TV.") The presentation of the instances was delayed because the child required a great deal of time to learn the specific response demanded by the first instance of a why question. The child required about ten times as long to master the first why question as the third. *In many ways the first why question was a sacrificial instance.* It required a far greater time to teach than the other instances and the chances of recurring mistakes are greater in response to the first than to any of the other instances. The reason is that the first instance had a far greater mistake potential than any of the other instances. The child had to learn the specific response of saying certain words. He also had to learn the "system" of cues that call for the particular response. The learning load is reduced on each of the subsequent instances, because the child is now required simply to give the appropriate response, not to learn a new set of conventions for responding.

The sacrificial instance presents a very real problem to the programmer. The first words that a child learns to read—*and, the, little, has*—require the greatest learning and are the most poorly retained. The first instance of a polar that a child learns, the first instance of "parts", materials, hierarchical classes—all are learned more slowly and retained more poorly. To teach the first instance, he must teach the "system" or the broader concept. But to teach the system is to increase the mistake potential.

There are three ways to solve the problem of the sacrificial instance. The first is to program a trivial instance—one that will not be used in the program. The object of this instance is to let the child work out his "system" errors on an instance that is not important. After he has mastered the trivial instance, the important instances can be introduced.

The second method involves presenting a first instance that is "easier" than those that are to follow. The mistake potential is reduced if the child makes fewer errors and learns more rapidly. If we want to teach naive children the concepts that reside in objects, we have a number of possible starting places. We can begin with colors, with prepositions, with polars, with materials, etc. There is actually no way of determining, through analysis of these instances of the broader concept, which will be easier for the child to learn. We must experiment. If our experimentation discloses that one of these concepts is easier to learn than the others, we would begin the program with that concept.

A third method for handling the sacrificial instance is to simplify the initial tasks if possible. Prepositions may be difficult for the child to master simply because the statements that describe positional relationships are involved. "The ball is over the chair." It may be possible, without inducing misrules, to "simplify" the statements during the initial presentation so that the child can master the concept more quickly. "We're talking about the ball. Is the ball over? Yes, the ball is over."

Cues in a Routine

To demonstrate that two things are the same, the teacher should demonstrate that they can be treated in the same way. However, if the demonstration is to work, the child must be able to see that she is treating them in the same way. The greater the number of points of similarity, the greater the possibility that the child will perceive that two instances are being treated in the same way. If the routine for a set of individual concepts is "unique", it has a general function with respect to other routines. The conversion becomes increasingly difficult. Conversely, the possibility that the child will learn that the instances of this routine are similar is increased because the possibility that he will fix on at least one of the points of similarity is increased. If there is only one point of similarity, the chances are slim. If there are eight points of similarity, the probability is increased substantially.

A cue is a unique signal or set of signals introduced to create a more general function with respect to two concepts that have specific-function relationship. If the concepts are similar, they are treated quite similarly; however, the similar treatment and the similar structure of the concepts implies that there will be difficult discriminations for the child. We can reduce the potential confusion by "making" these concepts less similar than they actually are. If we treat one in a unique way, we are exaggerating the dissimilarity of the concepts. We are increasing the probability that the child will be able to classify instances of the cued concept and note that they are the same. The instances of the concept that is not cued tend to be classified together on the basis of their similar treatment.

Cues are used effectively in almost all teaching situations. The teacher may "cue" one concept by working from a book while presenting instances of this concept. She presents instances of the other concept through demonstrations of real life objects. The teacher may use unique inflections when referring to all instances of the cued subject. She may introduce "Close your eyes. Can you tell if this ball is on the table? No. Okay, open your eyes . . ."

Note that the purpose of the cue is to reduce the possibility that the routine for a concept will be confused with other routines. The idea is to give the children the appropriate "set". As they learn to operate from the initial routine, the cues can be systematically dropped. If cues are dropped too rapidly, the children will tend to make mistakes. Their mistakes are a signal to return to the previous level of cues.

There is a difference between spurious cues and legitimate cues. Spurious cues are those that allow the child to produce the correct responses without following the operation implied by the task. Stated differently, a task contains spurious cues if the child responds to the *cue* not to the task. A spurious cue would be one in which the teacher presented the question and then moved her lips or shook her head to prompt the correct answer. While there are some tasks in which this procedure would be acceptable, it would not be acceptable for tasks in which the child is to arrive at the answer by performing a particular operation. *The presentation is not consistent with one and only one task-related concept.* The task is consistent with the task-related concept. "The way to discover the answer is to look at the teacher's face, not at the object presented."

The situation is quite different if the teacher introduces unique inflections in connection with a series of individual concepts. The inflection is a signal that the teacher is treating these instances in the same way. The inference is that there is a basis for sameness. This situation precisely parallels the situation in which the teacher refers to different instances with the same word. The steps that the child must take to answer the specific question presented have not changed. The child must conduct the same investigation that he would have to conduct if the teacher presented the question without cues.

Cues, Language and Efficiency

A teaching routine that can be generalized to process all of the concept instances to be taught is more efficient than a presentation that cannot be generalized. However, if we are given two routines that can be generalized, one may be more efficient than another. The more efficient routine will use language more economically and precisely, thereby reducing the error potential.

For example, the statement "This is a ball," is similar to the statement "This is red." The statements have the same general form. "This is ...." If a teacher uses this statement form to teach both the name of the object and the concept *red*, she is demonstrating to the child that both ball and red are instances of the same broad concept, as indeed they are. It is possible to "identify" a thing as either red or a ball. In both cases we must conduct an investigation to determine whether the thing actually has the characteristics of *ball* or of *red*.

However, *red* and *ball* are also different concepts. The routine that is used to process them must therefore do double duty. It must demonstrate the structure of the cluster by showing that although *red* and *ball* are instances of the same broader concept, *red* and *ball* are different in important respects. We could not readily convert the concept all into the concept red. Yet, a routine that treats these instances in basically the same way implies that the concepts have a specific function with respect to each other. (If we were teaching *ball* and *cat*, we would want to use the same routine, because the same task operation is implied—that of labelling the thing that is presented.)

The type of routine that is introduced to teach red should contain cues that alert the child to the fact that a different class of behavior is called for.

This is a ball.

This ball is red.

This pair of statements satisfies the requirement. The first statement identified the object. The second statement, which is different from the first, implies that the investigation to be conducted for redness has nothing to do with the object name. Since the object name is held constant in the second statement, the statement is saying in effect, "I know it's a ball, but it's also red." This point is made even more clearly when a variety of red objects is introduced.

Using the pair of statements also buttresses against different types of mistakes that the child may make. If the teacher presented the statement, "This is a red ball," instead of "This ball is red," it is possible for a child to point to a red truck and say, "This is not a red ball." The observation is correct but ambiguous. Does the child understand the concept red, or doesn't he? If the statement, "This ball is red," is presented, the child cannot make such a mistake. He cannot point to the truck and say, "This ball is not red," without revealing a conceptual problem.

A programmer never knows whether he has presented the most effective language routine that can be designed. He can point out that the routine (with variations) satisfies the requirements of the cluster that is to be taught, noting that there are cues for processing the individual concepts and cues that demonstrate how all instances in the cluster are instances of the same broader concept. He may further point out that the routine seems to involve "minimum language," with each operation expressed concisely in a single sentence and all of the elements in the statement performing a function (on either the level of the broader concepts or the individual concepts). However, he cannot declare that the routine is the most efficient one possible. Another routine may be produced which provides better cues, more effective design of the clusters, less language with greater language precision, etc. Another routine may buttress against more of the mistakes that children typically make in trying to learn the structure of the cluster.

Many questions of "efficiency" can be answered through analysis of the concept; however, others can be answered only after the program has been presented to children. As noted earlier, a program can specify the steps but it cannot indicate which of the steps will be relatively more difficult for the children to handle. It may be that a program will have to be revised on the basis of the children's performance. Additional steps may have to be taken in some parts (additional cues introduced and tasks simplified) and it may be possible to eliminate some of the steps. However, any revision must be in strict accordance with the principle: Priority must be given to the broader concepts; however, the routine must be adequate for demonstrating the individual concepts in the cluster.

Examples of Efficient Programs

Many of the examples used in this outline to illustrate the procedures of analysis and program construction have been oversimplified and abstracted from their program context. The reason is that many things happen in a program at the same time and examples of entire program sequences would probably prove to be "noisy" with irrelevant detail. In this section, we will study two programmed sequences in more detail. The descriptions of these programs are not complete; however, enough detail is provided so that the reader may observe the application of the principles that have been outlined so far. Note that there is actually very little noise in the programs. Every element in the routine and the presentation is justified according to one of the principles of teaching or sequencing.

Equality Example

The first program described in this section illustrates how individual concepts that are normally taught as discrete concepts can be treated as instances of a broader concept. This program is based on the idea that multiplication statements share a set of characteristics with the concept of balancing as it is used in lever problems and with the concept of numerical averaging. The potential efficiency of the program lies both in the generalization that results when

56

multiplication, lever problems, and averages are conceived of as instances of the same broad concept. An economy should also be realized in terms of the amount of time necessary to teach the different instances. Much of what is to be taught in connection with balance problems and averaging problems is programmed in connection with the first concept that is taught.

The program assumes that the children have already been taught multiplication as a process of counting by a number so many times. 5 x 4 involves counting by fives four times. The basic rule that will be used throughout the program is the equality rule: "As many as you have on one side, you have to have on the other, or the sides won't be equal. They won't balance."

The rule is first applied to balance problems. "As many as we have on this side of the balance, we have to have on this side of the balance." Note that the rule is almost identical to the equality rule. The cue that the lever problem is an instance of equality is therefore very strong.

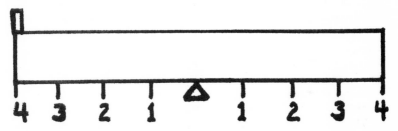

We put a weight at 4. We call this weight a *counter*. All counters are the same weight. We have one counter, so we have counted one time. We counted one time at four.

$$1 \times 4 =$$

"We counted to 4 on this side of the equal sign, so we must count to 4 on the other side. We know that four equals four." But we can assemble "four" in different ways. We can count one time at one and one time at three (which means that we put one weight at one and one weight at three).

$$1 \times 4 = 1 \times 1 + 1 \times 3$$

We can count two times at one and one time at two.

$$1 \times 4 = 2 \times 1 + 1 \times 2$$

We can count two times at two.

$$1 \text{ x } 4 = 2 \text{ x } 2$$

We can count one time at four.

$$1 \text{ x } 4 = 1 \text{ x } 4$$

We can count four times at one.

$$1 \text{ x } 4 = 4 \text{ x } 1$$

Or we can play a funny game in which we put some of the counters at zero. We can count five times at zero and one time at four.

$$1 \text{ x } 4 = 5 \text{ x } 0 + 1 \text{ x } 4$$

Through these exercises we demonstrate the basic laws of numbers.

The next step is to assign the child problems in which he is to count a specified number of times. The child is given four counters and is required to balance them in different ways and to write out the equation that describes each balance. He is asked whether each equation is true.

$$1 \text{ x } 3 + 1 \text{ x } 1 = 1 \text{ x } 0 + 1 \text{ x } 4$$

$$2 \text{ x } 3 = 1 \text{ x } 2 + 1 \text{ x } 4$$

In the next set of exercises, the child is asked to find the balance equal point. The rules are that *you must count at the equal point the same number of times you count at the other points on the board.*

If you count four times at different points on the board, that is the same as counting 4 times at the equal point, wherever that is.

Find the balance:

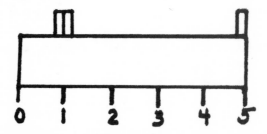

"How many times did we count? Four. Counting two times at one and two times at five is the same as counting four times at an unknown point. We can call that point b."

$$2 \times 1 + 2 \times 5 = 4 \times b$$
$$2 + 10 = 4b$$
$$12 = 4b$$
$$3 = b$$

The balance goes at 3.

After the children have worked a variety of similar problems with a variety of weight arrangements, they are introduced to different numbering scales on the board. The rule is that any scale will work so long as the intervals between the numbers are equal.

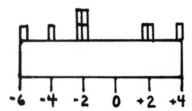

How many times did we count? Nine. So, counting one time at -6, one time at -4, one time at -2, two times at 2 and one time at 4 is the same as counting nine times at an unspecified point—b.

$$1 \times (\text{-}6) + 1 \times (\text{-}4) + 4 \times (\text{-}2) + 2 \times 2 + 1 \times 4 = 9b$$
$$(\text{-}6) + (\text{-}4) + (\text{-}8) + 4 + 4 = 9b$$
$$\text{-}10 = 9b$$
$$\frac{\text{-}10}{9} = b$$

One of the values of this kind of exercise is that it reinforces sign rules. If you were adding the counters on the minus side, the total must increase—the negative number must get bigger. Therefore, a minus times a plus must be a minus.

A following step involves the use of a scale that is based on an unspecified number, a.

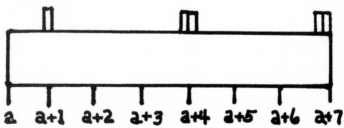

How many times do we count? Five. So:

$$1 \ (a + 1) + 2(a + 4) + 2(a + 7) = 5b$$
$$a + 1 + 2a + 8 + 2a + 14 = 5b$$
$$5a + 23 = 5b$$
$$\frac{5(a + 23)}{5} = 5b$$
$$a + \frac{23}{5} = b$$
$$a + 4\frac{3}{5} = b$$

Problems like the one above would be introduced only if the children had been taught the operation involved solving complex algebra problems. Various types of scales would be introduced (1a, 2a, 3a) (a/b, a/b + 1, a/b + 2).

Basic exercises with these scales can be used to demonstrate the logical necessity of algebraic conventions. For example, by having the children balance the board at n, they will see that what is true of number is true of notations like n + 4.

Balance the board by counting three times

$$1(n\text{-}2) + (n\text{-}1) + 1(n + 3) = 3n$$
$$n \text{ - } 2 + n \text{ - } 1 + n + 3 = 3n$$
$$3n = 3n$$

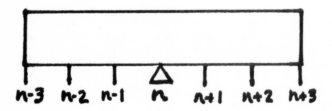

n-3   n-2   n-1   n   n+1   n+2   n+3

If the board balances, the children will always arrive at an answer similar to this. The basic truth is that if things are equal, they are numerically the same.

Averaging problems are presented next. The teaching routine is similar to the routine used to demonstrate balancing.

"On the average, how many glasses of water does John drink in a day. Let's mark the scale off in number of glasses."

One day, John drinks four glasses. So we put a counter at four. We count one time at four. One day, he drinks three glasses, so we count one time at 3. One day he drinks 8 glasses. And on *three days* he drinks 5 glasses. How many times are we counting at five? Three times. He did it three days.

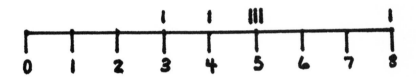

How many times do we count? Six. So we can balance these numbers. It's the same as counting six times at an unspecified point.

$$1 \times 3 + 1 \times 4 + 3 \times 5 + 1 \times 8 = 6b$$
$$30 = 6b$$
$$5 = b$$

"On the average, John drank five glasses of water a day."

The final steps in the program involve different scales and the application of averaging to different types of situations. Note that the teaching routine for averaging problems is quite similar to that used to teach the balance principle, which means that the probability of a child seeing that all are instances of the same concept is increased. Both the lever principle and the averaging principle can be expanded. The principles of all simple machines can be taught using a variation of the balance problem (specifying distance from the balance and then determining how many times one will have to count to balance a given product). A host of statistical operations are built upon the averaging routine that has been programmed.

The program outlined above did not spring from intuition. If anything, it was created against the natural inclinations of the author, who probably learned the discrete concepts of levers and averaging in the same way the reader did. An analysis of the balance concept and the averaging concept disclosed that they shared a set of characteristics. These characteristics were programmed, using a routine (with variations) that would allow for the processing of each instance.

The sequence of the tasks in the program was dictated by the structure of the individual concepts taught (balancing and averaging). We can demonstrate balancing. We can show the children that a board will balance if we balance the counters according to the rules of equality. When we deal with numerical averages, however, we can't provide a very compelling demonstration that we have actually achieved an average. Uusually, the child must take the teacher's word for it. He is told simply that if he adds the total and divides by the number of events, he will have the average. But there is no way that a teacher can show the child that he has created something called an average, in the way that one can create a balance.

Balance problems are therefore introduced first. These are processed with a highly cued routine. When the same routine is used to process problems involving averaging, the child has reason to believe that the procedure works. He had received compelling demonstrations that the procedure works; it therefore follows that it will work on all problems that have the same characteristics as balance problems. Since the routine for balancing was used to process averaging problems, the child was given strong evidence that both instances could be treated in the same way and therefore must be the same so far as their operational characteristics are concerned.

If the program had started with averaging problems (as many school problems do) the child would have been required to learn the averaging rule without receiving a strong demonstration that it worked. Later, he would encounter lever problems, the teaching routine for which would have a general function with respect to the averaging routine. The shared characteristic of linear equations, averaging problems, and lever problems would therefore not be made explicit. The child would have no reason to classify these problems together. He would tend to see them as instances of the same problem because he would not have been taught that they are instances of the same concept and can be expressed with the same routine.

Piling Up Example

This program illustrates how it often is possible to program elementary concepts in such a way that they are consistent with more technical concepts. The concept programmed is that of geological time. An examination of the concept discloses that our knowledge of geological time is based on inferences, not direct observation. The basis of inference is the broad concept that is programmed first because it is the very characteristic that all instances of geological time share.

We first introduce the rule: "When things pile up they go this way." ↑ Next we demonstrate the rule. We place an object on the floor. We then place another object on top of it. Every time we place another object we relate the situation to the rule. "Things are piling up. Which way are they going?"

For demonstrating the implications of the rule we present a pile of things and ask the children which object was put in the pile first, which object next. If the children have trouble, we demonstrate how the pile had been constructed. We make another pile that is identical to the first. "Which is coming first? . . . Yes, the red block. And then which one comes next? . . . Yes, the pile is going this way . . . So the first one is always on the bottom".

After the children have demonstrated that they can handle tasks similar to the one above, we present a series of "detective games", in which the children are told stories such as, "You go to the park and you see this pile of things."

The things are identified as part of a hamburger, part of an ice cream cone and a gum wrapper. "Somebody ate lunch and just threw the stuff on the ground. Can you figure out what he ate first?"

The format of the problem is then changed. "You dig a hole in the ground and here's what you find."

"Can you tell me which was put in the hole first? . . . Remember, the rule: when things pile up they go this way . . . ".

The children are presented with a variety of similar problems, including problems in which they encounter different layers when they dig a hole—a sand layer, a layer of shells, a layer of pebbles. The questions that are presented are always the same and the same rule is used to arrive at the answer. When things pile up, they go this way.

The next step in the program involves a further expansion of the rule. The children are presented with questions about time. "Was the shoe put here the same time as the can? Was the shoe put here the same time as the box?" A variation of the question, "If the shoe and the can were put here at the same time, show me where the can should be . . . Yes, on the same place in the pile as the can."

The final step in the program is that of relating the rules to geological evidence. This step is a simple extension of what the children have already learned. Before the relationships are drawn, the children are taught about skeletons, fossils, and the tendency of streams to deposit material or create piles of sand. Then they are taught the rule:

If two things are the same "level" or in the same strata, they were put in the pile at the same time. If not on the same level they were not put in the pile at the same time.

The basis of the routine for teaching geological time is the principle of piling. The program starts with this rule because it can be demonstrated and because it can be observed in everyday life. The routine is established in such a way that geological problems would be treated as instances of the more general piling concept. The cues in the program are designed to prompt children to think about geological time in terms of piling, not the passage of time. We cannot expect the child to "extrapolate" from his temporal experience and arrive at an intuitive understanding of one hundred and thirty million years. We can, however, expect him to appreciate the steps that geological investigators go through before indicating that dinosaurs lived milions of years ago and that there were no men on earth at that time. The geological investigator concludes that there were no men because there were no remains of men in the piles that he has observed.

It is possible to demonstrate other important concepts using the core that had already been programmed about time. For example, time lines can be introduced to demonstrate that if the rate of which a line is drawn up is held constant, the passage of time is marked off in equal intervals. (The line moves up in the same way the pile grows).

Comment

Efficient programs are not created by chance. The statements in a routine are not dictated by the grammarian or the armchair philosopher who supposes that he "knows" the concept that is being taught. Routines are not dictated by the illustrations in the program that must have captions. Priorities are not established by copying other programs. The substance of the program derives primarily from the concept clusters that are being programmed. The name of the game is to demonstrate the structure of the cluster in such a way that the child will be able to "generalize" from the individual concepts that are taught to the broader concept that encompasses all instances within the cluster. The program starts here—not with tasks or responses.

The focus of this chapter is on program efficiency, because efficiency seems to be the most important question in education. The question, "Can you teach this child to read at the fourth-grade level by the time he enters the fourth grade?" is far more relevant than the question, "Can you teach this child to read?" What have we demonstrated if we teach him to read? Probably very little. But if we can demonstrate that we can accelerate the rate at which he is taught, we demonstrate that our program has important educational implications. The program not only works; it is technically superior to other programs.

Not all of the techniques used to achieve program efficiency were outlined on the preceding pages. Rather, the discussion focused to the problem of using routines to cue a child so that he can learn concept clusters more rapidly. The primary technique demonstrated was that if things are treated in the same way, the child is given a basis for classifying the things together. This does not mean that he will be able to give the teacher a verbal explanation that he is learning clusters. He will be able to demonstrate what he has learned by applying the routines that have been programmed.

The expected product of efficient programs is (a) that children who have gone through the program will be able to perform more effectively on the level of the individual concepts as well as the level of the broader concept; and (b) that the skills in the program can be taught in less time because less teaching is involved.

CHAPTER VI

PROBLEM SOLVING

Problems As Tasks

When we begin to analyze what is meant by "problem solving", we note that problems are quite similar to tasks. Both problems and tasks involve operations. Both imply some kind of acceptable responses. Both are irreducible signals to engage in a particular form of behavior. And both are composed of component elements—words or symbols that have a "public" meaning of some sort. It is sometimes suggested that a problem is the chaining of concepts, but where does the chaining start? Is "Throw the ball to daddy" a problem or a task? If it is a task, how do we classify an event in which the child is given an object and instructed to "Throw"? One of these tasks seems to have more parts and involve a longer chain of concepts than the other. If "Throw the ball to daddy" is a task, what do we call "Close your eyes; turn around three times; and see if you can throw the ball to Daddy without opening your eyes"? There seems to be what we might call problem-solving behavior in this problem, but are the problem solving requirements of this task of a different "form" than those of the preceding tasks?

Problem-solving forms a legitimate class if techniques for teaching problem-solving differ from those used to teach tasks. They don't, but they often involve more elaborate applications of task-programming.

When we tell a child to "look at this" as we present something, we are presenting a sample task. But in order for him to perform, *he has to solve a problem.* He is given a criterion by which to measure his performance. To solve the problem he has to do something consistent with the instructions, "Look at this." He has to isolate that which he should look at from all of the other things that are within his visual field.

How is he able to extract from the words that are given what kind of operation is called for? What cues does he receive to let him know that he should look at only one of the various objects that are within his visual field? There are cues in the presentation and cues in the signal that is given. But what are these cues? Similar questions can be asked about any problem or any task. We cannot give an epistomological answer or a physiological answer to why a child learns to solve problems and handle complex tasks. But the educational answer is quite simple. The child is taught.

We know that children are "individually different." We know that two children will probably require a different amount of practice to learn the generalization. It is therefore absurd to assume that if two children are exposed to the same physical presentation, they will perform in the same way on a test of what they have been taught. However, *if both of these children are brought to a specified criterion of performance in a program that is designed to teach the concept, we would expect both of them to pass the test.* The concept—or generalization—can be taught. This is the basic assumption of teaching. To learn the concept, the child must learn about the concept's characteristics, regardless of whether this child has an IQ of 34 or 134. The differences in these children are measurable, but the differences in no way change the teaching requirements implied by the concept. Both children must be taught the same operations. Both must be taught to respond to the same cues. Both must go through the same process of discovering the rule from the teaching routines. The program for both is the same program with the same criteria, the same set of sub skills. One child may already have been taught important components of the program. One child may proceed through the program more rapidly than the other. But there is no way that a child can "learn" a concept without learning the characteristics of that concept. There is no way a child can handle a task without learning to respond to the signals in the task. Yes, there are individual differences in children, and yes, there would be program variations for the child who is able to move faster and for the child who has already been taught some of the operations called for by the problem. But to assume that one child can "generalize" without having been *taught* the concept that is being applied to different instances is as absurd, from the standpoint of teaching technology, as assuming that a child can learn to walk, learn the English language, and learn such concepts as *chair* without being taught.

Problem-Solving and Intent

A great deal of the confusion associated with problem-solving stems from the question of *intent*. What is a particular problem designed to demonstrate? Often an examination of a problem does not imply a program, because the intent of the problem may be quite different from what we might suppose it is. Consider the familiar water-transfer problem. A child is shown two identical glasses, both filled with water to the same level. The child indicates that they have the same amount. Now, the contents of one of the glasses is transferred to a glass that is much wider. The child is asked to compare the liquid in the wider glass and the original glass that still contains water.

Let's say that we were given this task and asked to write a program for 5-6 year old children who fail it. Our attack would be to note the possible sources of error (confusion of same level with same amount, etc.) and to identify the "key" concept. We would do this by assuming that a child would fail a similar task in which confusion of level and amount would not be a source of error if he had not been taught the "key concept". In fact, we could construct an indefinite number of tasks involving the key concept, and the child would fail all of them. We might decide that this key concept is that water does not expand and shrink. The units are fixed.

The program that we would devise to demonstrate this concept would involve first a compelling demonstration that regardless of the configurational changes of a given amount of water, the amount remains the same. We might initially present two identical closed

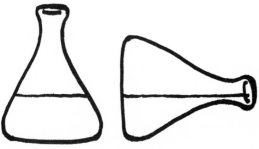

69

containers, both containing the same amount of water—one container on its side and the other standing upright.

After asking the child which contains more water, we would stand up the container that had been on its side. We would continue to change the positions of the containers, demonstrating that they "look" the same when they are both on their sides, and when they are both rightsideup. Therefore, they must be the same when they don't look the same.

Next we would repeat the same demonstration starting with a different amount in each of the containers. Whenever the containers are in the same position, the original relationship obtain. The vessel that originally contained more liquid still contains more liquid. The various transformations in shape that are observed as the vessel changes positions are demonstrated to be irrelevant. When both vessels are in the same position, the original relationship holds.

This program would work. We don't have to experiment with children to know that it will work. It has to work. And the program legitimately teaches the concept that we have identified—water has fixed units of amount. Note that the children were not presented with the water-transfer problem in the training. They were not taught to *pass the test*. Rather, they were taught to pass an indefinite number of tests that involve the concept. We would therefore expect them to be able to solve the test problem and various other problems involving this concept.

Our programming efforts, however, may be met with the reaction, "So what?" Although we did an honest job of task analysis, starting with the task that was given and then programming the components, we did not consult the *intent* of those who had developed the test. This task, we may be told, was not designed to test the children's ability to handle water transfer problems as such. It was designed to test a concept much broader. That concept tested, they may tell us, is "compensation reasoning", or the notion that if the units of something are "fixed," any change in the original configuration must be compensated for by another configurational change. Our critics may point out that the children who received our training actually learned something rote about water. They did not learn compensation reasoning. To demonstrate the point, our critics may present children who have gone through our program with two identical balls of clay. After deforming one of the balls into a long sausage, they ask "Does one of these have more clay now?" Some of the children will probably fail this test. Our critics will take this failure as evidence that we did not actually teach the children the "concept" of which the water-transfer problem was an instance.

70

The Size of the Cluster

However, if we had known the intent of the problem, *we would have changed the size of the concept cluster to be programmed.* The water-transfer problem is an instance of the concept that water doesn't expand. And, it is also an instance of the concept that compensating changes occur if the units are fixed. The difference between the concept that we chose as the basis for our program and the compensating-change concept is that the compensating change concept has a larger range of positive instances. All of the water-level problems that we identified are positive instances, and additional instances that were not included in our group of concept instances are also included.

The concept of compensating changes involves a larger cluster than *water-as-fixed units.* Since it involves a different cluster, it implies a different program. The demonstration instances must now be selected according to the requirements of the broader concept. A routine that allows us to treat all instances in the same way (according to the compensation rule) must be introduced. The program that we develop must derive from our analysis of the concept. But unless we know what the concept is that we are trying to teach, we may either identify a concept that is too narrow or too broad.

The Floating Standard

Often the only way to determine the size of the cluster that should be programmed is to have the author of a task or series of tasks *specify a range of other tasks that the child who had been taught the concept would be able to handle.* This procedure provides us with a kind of operational definition of the cluster. If the tasks are diverse (such as solving displacement problems and solving water-transfer problems) a relatively large cluster is implied. The shared characteristic of these problems is that they are both instances of the rule: the units put in equal the units removed. This rule applies to a substantial range of problems.

Unless we receive some information about the size of the cluster, the critic can use a floating standard to evaluate the outcome of training. He does this by shifting from one cluster to another. "Yes", he may acknowledge, "the children can perform *that* task, but what about *this* task." He then presents a task not included in the original cluster. The critic may note that a five-year old child who has been taught to handle numerical multiplication problems cannot handle story problems that reduce to multiplication. The program may not have been designed to teach story problems. The initial cluster may have involved only the basic formal operation as it applies to the regrouping and counting of objects. However, the critics may suppose that he has leveled a devastating criticism by finding a problem that the children cannot solve. If the problem had been within the concept cluster that had been taught, the finding would have been devastating. To discover an instance from another cluster, however is not particularly damaging or puzzling.

The confusion that some educators have about problem solving stems from their reluctance to look at concepts analytically. The floating standard and the general mystique connected with "problem solving behavior" is the product of an amorphous understanding of what teaching is and how teaching programs derive. Some educators may note that the water level is an instance of compensation reasoning or of simultaneous changes of two dimensions of an object, but they have difficulty appreciating that the same problem is also an instance of other concepts, some of which are broader and others of which are narrower. Unless the size of the cluster is clearly understood, no systematic program can be constructed.

Programming Problem Solving Behavior

The general procedure for developing a problem-solving program begins with broad task analysis (outlined in Chapter 4). The programmer begins with the assumption that *the test problem is an instance of similar problems or tasks.* All are instances of a concept. It follows that if the child is taught the shared characteristics of the concept and the task-related concepts embedded in the task, the child should be able to handle the test problem, even though this problem is not presented in the training. The stipulation that the problem should not have been presented in the training is crucial to problem solving, because the primary goal of problem-solving programs is to demonstrate that what has been taught to the class of positive instances can be applied to any individual instance within the class. To repeat a point made several times in this section: the purpose of training is not to teach for a specific task, but to teach for an indefinite number of tasks that share unique characteristics.

Assuming that there is some agreement on the size of the cluster that is to be tested, the programmer can begin to write a program that teaches the structure of the cluster. The procedures for this type of programming have been outlined in the preceding chapter. A strong routine is needed to demonstrate that the instances within the class are to be treated in the same way. The need for an effective routine becomes urgent as problems become increasingly complex and as the child must work with longer chains of reasoning to arrive at the appropriate solution. Often the child cannot "see" that the instances are the same. Often, the problem-solving procedure serves as proof that an instance has certain characteristics. The child cannot "see" that averaging problems are instances of balancing. If the balancing routine holds for averaging problems, however, averaging problems must be instances of balancing. Stated another way: the child is taught a routine. He receives demonstrations that the routine "works" when it is applied to particular problems. The basic principle is that if instances can be treated in the same way, they are instances of the same concept. He then encounters other instances. To discover whether or not they are instances of the familiar concept, he uses the routine. If no contradiction results, they are instances of the concept. The routine becomes the criterion for classifying concepts. If the routine is inadequate for processing the range of instances, the child will not discover that the full range of instances share certain characteristics. He will be limited in his approach by his criterion.

If the instances to be processed with a given routine had a general function with respect to all concepts, the programmer's job would be easy. But often the class of positive instances share no obvious set of characteristics. (Balancing problems are not perceptibly similar to averaging problems.) The programmer must therefore make the concept instances more uniform and at the same time less similar to not-instances. This goal is best achieved by introducing a very strong routine that is applied to a range of problems that vary widely in perceptible properties.

Another Water-Transfer Program

The relationship between the program, the routine, and the size of the concept cluster that is identified can be illustrated by the following program. The author noted that water-transfer problems are actually similar to rectangle problems, and that the principles of fixed units of water can be demonstrated nicely with rectangles. Water-transfer problems and rectangular transformations are instances of the same concept. According to this analysis, the water transfer problem is included in an "unlikely" cluster.

The author wanted to demonstrate through a program for teaching water-transfer skills that some of the assumptions about how children learn about water transfer are wrong. Some have suggested that in order to learn about water transfer a child must (a) manipulate water, and (b) observe the actual transformation as water is transferred from one container to one of a different width. The author decided to develop a program in which the child would neither deal with water nor observe the "process" of changing shape as water is transferred.

The author had placed rather severe limitations on the program. He could not demonstrate forms of the original problem (which means he could not use a program similar to the one outlined on p. 69). He could not refer to water transfer. He had to work from "rectangles" and use a strong routine to relate rectangular glasses with other rectangles, so that the rules taught about other rectangles would "transfer" to water. Such transfer can be induced because such transfer is logically possible.

If it is true that water level problems involving "rectangular-like" glasses are instances of a larger cluster of rectangle problems and if it is true that the characteristics of the larger class are shared by the water-transfer problems, it is possible to treat all of these instances in the same way. The key to this program's success lies in the effectiveness of the routine that "increases" the similarity among the positive instances of the concept. The routine must cue the children to view glasses of water as rectangles.

The Program

The first set of exercises is designed to demonstrate the independence of size and amount. Children are introduced to problems in which both rectangular and nonrectangular diagrams are presented.

"These are pockets. Which pocket is bigger? . . . Which pocket has more pieces of bubble gum in it?" . . . Included in these examples are representations of glasses, the only glasses represented in the program. Note, however, that the glasses are the same width and the question has nothing to do with transfer of water.

"These are two glasses. Which glass is taller? . . . Which glass has more water in it?"

By introducing a variety of instances and applying the same routine, we are implying that the principle we are teaching applies to a wide range of instances, including glasses.

Next the principle that rectangles are composed of "fixed units" is provided. The rule for any initial demonstration is that is must be "provable." The children must be able to see that the rule being introduced works. They must not be expected to take the teacher's word for it. The demonstration: while the children cannot observe what we are doing, we trace around a rectangular eraser, first as it is oriented vertically and then horizontally. We ask the children which rectangle is "bigger". After they indicate that the vertically oriented rectangle is bigger, we act amused and tell them that the rectangles are the same size. We prove our point by placing the eraser over the vertical rectangle and then over the horizontal rectangle. We now present the basic problem-solving rule. We refer to the change in height by saying "Look at these two boxes. What happened to the box this way when we tipped it over?" Yes, it got shorter." Referring to the width we say "And what happened to the box this way when we turned it over? . . . It got longer."

The rule: "If it gets longer this way (height), it has to get shorter this way (width)." Throughout the program we will use variations of this rule. We have the children repeat it and repeat the other variation. (If the height gets shorter, the width gets longer.) Note that the rule refers to change: "If it *gets* shorter . . .". The rule anticipates the test problem.

The children are next shown how the rule applies to block piling. This demonstration is compelling because the children can apply the rule and continue to receive "proof" that it works. We introduce a diagram showing a row of twelve blocks.

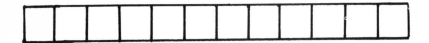

After the children have counted the blocks, we introduce the rule about changing the shape of rectangles and ask the children to use the rule to predict. This is an important step in programming that has not been previously discussed. Initially, a rule is introduced *after* it has been demonstrated. Later, the rule is moved to what we might call a "predictive" position in our routine. The children must now use the rule as a basis for predicting outcomes. We don't expect them to actually "learn" the rule from our initial demonstrations. We do expect them to note that it was derived from a demonstration and to anticipate that this rule will be used.

"I'm going to make this pile of blocks shorter this way (indicating width). What's going to happen to the pile this way (indicating height)?" Answer: It will get longer. "Yes, let's all say the rule: If it gets shorter this way, it has to get longer this way."

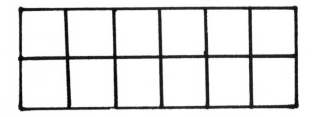

"Was the rule right?" I made the pile shorter this way, so it had to get longer this way." Note that the problem deals with a fixed number of blocks, but the rule has no mention of number. The reason is that we want the child to apply the rule beyond the range of things that can be counted. The rule is a rule about shape. However, we are using the counters because we want the child to associate rectangles with fixed units.

We tell the children that we are going to rearrange the blocks again. Indicating the width we say, "We're going to make this pile of blocks shorter this way. What's going to happen this way? . . . Yes, it will get longer." We erase four blocks from the end of the pile and draw them on top of the pile.

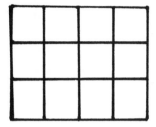

"Did the rule work?" We continue repiling the blocks until we have a single vertical column of twelve blocks. Then we ask the children "What would happen if I took this pile of blocks and tipped it over on its side? What would happen this way? . . . And what would happen this way? . . . Yes, if it gets longer this way, it has to get shorter this way." Note that this final exercise in the series relates the block-piling exercises to the eraser demonstration. We are telling the child that if the amount of matter remains the same, whether the matter is rearranged or simply tipped, the same rule applies.

We work on variations of the block piling task until the children are able to apply the rule consistently. Then we introduce the final set of tasks in the series—painting on a flat surface. The purpose of these exercises is to relate our rule to substances in which the counters are not blocks or other perceptible counters.

We present the children with two rectangles that have the same height but different widths.

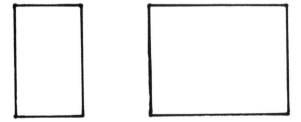

Problem: "We have just enough paint to paint the narrow rectangle. How far up would we be able to paint the wide rectangle?" We introduce a painting convention. To paint a rectangle, we have to go from side to side, starting at the bottom.

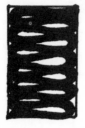 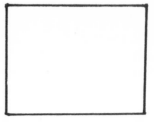

"There. I painted this box. Now you've got the same amount of paint to paint the other box. Show me how far you can paint."

If a child paints all the way to the top of the wider rectangle, we ask him, "What's the rule? Look at these patches you painted. Look what happened. It got longer this way (width). If it gets longer this way, it has to do what? . . . Yes, gets shorter the other way. Did your patch get shorter the other way? . . . No. So did you use the same amount of paint I used? . . . No. You used more paint. But you don't have more paint".

A variety of similar painting problems is introduced, and the children are asked to apply the rule to each. In some problems, the rectangles differ in both height and widths. For one variation, we paint both rectangles to the top and then ask the children if we used the same amount of paint. We then ask them to show about where we have stopped painting.

After the children have demonstrated that they can handle the painting problems, we introduce the water-transfer problem and note whether or not they pass it.

The program described above was administered to fifteen children who could not handle the water level problem on a pretest (Englemann, 1967). These children were matched with control children who did not receive training. After training (which required 54 minutes, distributed over a school week), ten of the fifteen experimental children passed the water level problem and were able to solve problems that involved manipulating a two-dimensional model. The model displayed two "glasses." A movable strip could be raised and lowered, giving the impression that the liquid level in the glasses was being changed. The investigator would set the level of the narrower glass and then ask the children how much more juice the other glass would have if the contents of the investigator's glass were transferred into the other.

None of the children in the control group was able to pass the tasks on water transfer.

The program was not a complete success. Not all of the children who received training passed the criterion problems. Before this program is readministered to children, the programmer should examine it in detail to try to discover where it is weak. Why did some of the children fail? Did they fail to learn the basic rules about rectangles or did they fail to transfer this rule to the water-transfer problem? Which of the sub-skills in the program was not adequately taught? The answers to these questions can be discovered by analyzing the performance of the children in more detail. The original program was written without ever first working with children. It was devised according to the programming principles outlined in this book. But, as noted previously, these procedures do not indicate which sub-skills are difficult and which area easy. It may be that more time must be spent on the basic set of exercises in which the independence of size and amount is demonstrated. If this is the case, a further analysis of these tasks is implied and more detailed instruction is implied.

Despite the shortcomings of the program, it demonstrates that a unique cluster like the rectangle cluster can be identified. If the test problem is actually an instance of "rectangular-like transformation," then it is possible to treat the problem as an instance of this cluster and develop a program that articulates the characteristics that the problem shares with other instances within the cluster. The program further demonstrated conclusively (not merely statistically) that the developmental assumptions about how children learn about water transfer are incorrect. Children are taught. They don't have to be shown actual water transfer; they don't have to manipulate. They have to learn a basic rule about the property of water. In the present program they learned a broader rule, for experimental reasons only. They learned about transformations with rectangles. Most of them were able to transfer what they had learned to water transfer problems.

The procedures from which the present program was generated are the same as those for programming any concept cluster:

(1) Specify the cluster that is to be taught. Without precise specification, none but an intuitive and perhaps lucky program is possible. Do not suppose that there will be uniform transfer outside of the cluster. The program will not be designed to teach skills outside of the cluster. Note that a given problem does not "automatically" imply a given cluster. It may imply a number of different clusters, each of which would describe a different program.

(2) Develop a routine that allows for the processing of all instances within the cluster. The routine must demonstrate that all instances can be treated in the same way.

(3) Select a range of demonstration instances from within the cluster. If one selects instances that share too many characteristics, a possible misrule will be learned. All irrelevant characteristics must be "factored out" through demonstrations that the routine applies to instances that do not have these characteristics.

(4) Use presentational cues that facilitate the transfer to the task on which the children will be tested. In the water-transfer program there were a number of cues that were similar to the cues presented in the test problem. For example, the convention for "painting" was similar to the way in which water is poured into a container, starting at the bottom and then moving up a level at a time. Also, the arrangement of the rectangles was similar, with the narrower rectangle on the left and the wider rectangle on the right. The purpose of the cues is to make divergent problems as similar as possible, to create a class of instances that has a general function with respect to other instance.

(5) Begin with demonstrations that relate to concepts the child has already learned. Don't start with demonstrations that are valid in terms of what the child knows. Derive the rule or routine from these demonstrations and then apply the rule to other instances that are not as easily proven.

(6) Adhere to the principles of adequacy and economy in constructing teaching routines for the concepts that are to be used in the program. Make the concept presentation unambiguous, so that it is consistent with one and only one concept.

CHAPTER VII

PROGRAMMING REINFORCEMENT

A task implies that the child must learn a particular discrimination and express his awareness of the discrimination by using the signal specified by the task. According to the structure of tasks, the child must produce some kind of response. But why should the child do what we want him to do? Perhaps we are asking him to perform actions and conduct investigations that are difficult. Why should he bother? He may find more enjoyment in doing something else.

From the standpoint of teaching the answer is: *the child will perform the actions that are specified by the task only if he receives a greater pay-off for these behaviors than he does for other types of behavior that are available to him at the moment.* This does not mean that all learning is necesarily contingent upon reinforcement. It does mean, however, that if we want to teach the child something, we have to use contingent reinforcement. Only through the use of contingencies can we be assured of controlling the child's behavior. According to the reinforcement principle, we can get the desired response by introducing a stronger payoff. Children may learn in a number of ways. They may learn without ever producing responses. They may learn whether or not they are reinforced. However, they cannot be consistently *taught* unless the reinforcing variables are controlled.

When a child is taught a particular task, he must learn that concept that is involved, the rule for responding, *and the rule that the response will produce an outcome that is desired by the child.* Unless the child learns the third part of this equation, we have no way of knowing whether or not he has learned the other two parts. This means that the task must be structured in such a way that there is a relative pay-off for performing. The child must learn the rule that "for me, trying to produce the response is worth the effort." The effort may be quite great. In other words, what we ask the child to do may be "punishing". We must compensate for the punishment.

This point is very important. The child may learn both the concept we are trying to teach and the rule for performing. But this learning is not enough. He must also learn that he will receive something that he wants if he responds. The emphasis is on *wants*. The teaching that is implied in any task situation is to demonstrate this concept or rule: "You will get something you want only if you perform." We will return to this point shortly.

Reinforcement is used non-contingently as well as contingently in a well-designed program. The reason is that we want to reduce the degree of punishment that is inherent in the teaching presentation. If a demonstration contains reinforcing elements (things that are fun to watch and do), the amount of punishment is reduced. (These demonstration elements are non-contingent because they are presented whether or not the child produces the desired types of orienting responses, etc. However, they do not have to be non-contingent. If the demonstration or task is "reinforcing," which means that the children give behavioral indications that they choose that task over other events that are available to them, the teacher can tell the children that they will be able to work that task or see that demonstration only if they perform on another task. One of the major problems associated with the presentation of non-contingent reinforcers is that there is always the possibility that the children will become entertained by these reinforcers without learning the basic discriminations that the teacher is trying to teach. As a rule, initial demonstrations should be reasonably clean and have a minimum of non-contingent reinforcers that are not functional in establishing a routine or teaching concept discriminations.

Generally, *non-contingent reinforcement is used most effectively in the demonstration of the concept.* In other words, the presentation is made interesting. *Contingent reinforcement is used most effectively to structure the tasks so that the child is compensated for the amount of punishment that may be inherent in task performance.*

Reinforcement As Concept Teaching

Earlier we noted that a given teaching presentation may be consistent with more than one concept. If a teacher holds up an apple and says, "This is red," her presentation is consistent with the concept she is trying to teach, but it is also consistent with other concepts. The word red could have many meanings. Her presentation may also demonstrate an unintended concept that has nothing to do with red. She may present the apple to a child and say, "What is this?" The child answers, "Apple." Teacher: "But what color is it? . . . Is is red?" Child: "I don't know." Teacher: Look at it. Is is red?" Child shrugs and looks down. The teacher did not intend to demonstrate to the child that he is a failure, that he is dumb, or that learning is a punishing experience. However, her presentation is quite consistent with these concepts. She presented the child with an instance of failure in the learning situation. If she presents a number of similar demonstrations, we would expect the child to learn about the characteristics of a new-learning situation just as certainly as we would expect him to learn any other concept the instances of which are systematically presented. If the child is shown that every instance of new learning has a unique set of shared characteristics, he will "learn the rule."

The principles for teaching generalizations are the same for concepts that are independent of content as they are for content concepts. The teacher can induce a generalization by treating a wide variety of instances in the same way, thereby demonstrating that all of these instances have the same set of characteristics. If the teacher demonstrates that all instances of "new learning" share the same set of failure characteristics, the child will learn that he is a failure in new-learning situations — a more general concept. If the teacher demonstrates that only certain tasks within the new learning situation have failure characteristics, the child will learn that he is a failure at only some new-learning situations—a specific concept. In every case, the generalization that is taught is a function of the group of instances that is presented.

Reinforcing Variables in Every Teaching Demonstration

It is impossible to demonstrate any concept without also teaching a concept about the act of learning. The reason is simply that it is impossible to teach without introducing a teaching presentation. Every teaching demonstration has characteristics that relate the child to the teaching presentation. "The material is dull to me." "Every time I say something, I get punished." "I like arithmetic." "I have to work hard but it's worth it because I can really use whatever I learn." The rules can be very narrow or very broad. They can deal with a particular task, a set of tasks, all school learning, or some component of a task.

The analysis of rules that relate the child to the teaching encounter is difficult because the presentation of these rules operates on a completely different wave length than the concept presentation. Yet, both the programming of concepts about the teaching demonstration and about specific concepts must be conducted simultaneously. The only instances of concepts about teaching demonstrations are teaching demonstrations. The teaching demonstration itself (the routines, tasks, and teacher reactions to the child's performance) are the events that generate the concepts.

What this means is that while a teacher's presentation may satisfy the teaching requirements outlined in the preceding chapters, it may be an instance of an unintended concept. The teacher may do a perfect job of demonstrating what the concept *chair* is. She may provide a demonstration that is consistent only with one interpretation. Yet, she may demonstrate the content-independent concept, "I am not satisfied with your performance." This concept is independent of the concept that is being taught because it is possible to create another demonstration that teaches the same content concept (chair) and at the same time present an instance of a concept that is incompatible with the concept, "I am not satisfied with your performance," (I *am* quite satisfied with your performance.) A given teaching demonstration contains instances of many "content-independent" concepts. For example, the teacher says, "Tell me the word and I'll show you the picture. Listen: mmmmmaaaaannnnn. Say it fast . . . What word is that? . . . Good . . . You're really smart. What are you going to see in the picture? . . . "

The presentation is consistent with a number of concepts that relate the child to the teaching encounter. For example, "There is a pay-off for responding correctly." "School work is fun." "The teacher is a nice lady." "I got to see the picture because I am smart."

Concepts about the teacher, about the material, about the significance of the work that is done in school, about the child's adequacy are taught like any other concepts. Instances are presented. Perhaps these instances are described with a verbal rule, but even if a verbal rule is presented, it usually must be backed up with instances of the concept. These concepts are taught whether they are taught accidentally or as part of a programmed sequence. When they are taught accidently, however, the possibility is great that the teacher is not actually teaching what she wants to teach. She may want to let the child know that he should work harder, and instead of presenting instances of the concept, "There is a pay-off for hard work," she scolds the child and gives him a great deal of attention for not working hard. When he tries to work, she acts as if she *expects* such behavior, "That's a little better, Tom." Perhaps she wonders why the child does not perform well in school.

Teaching Content-Independent Concepts

The introduction of content-independent concepts into a program changes the program. The basic requirements imposed by the content that is being taught do not change. We do not derive programs from our need to provide effective reinforcers. We derive them from the concepts that we wish to teach. The content concepts take precedent. Content-independent concepts are then programmed into the basic framework implied by the content concepts. (Remember, content-independent concepts are independent of the content and can therefore be programmed into any sequence, including those that are not effective in teaching the desired content concept. Therefore, we cannot use content-independent concepts as a guide for deciding how to teach content concepts.)

With the introduction of content-independent concepts, the teaching demonstration must perform jobs simultaneously. It must demonstrate the structure of the content concept, and it must also teach the child the content-independent concept that we wish to teach. The teaching demonstration itself must be an instance of "I can succeed if I work hard," "I am smart," "learning is fun," or whatever content-independent concept we wish to teach. The changes that are necessary in the original teaching demonstration to teach the desired content-independent concepts:

1. must not distract from the presentation of the content concept;

2. must provide the child with a clean instance of the concept-independent concept that is being taught, eg., it must provide a clear instance of "If you work hard you will get a pay-off," "You are a smart boy," etc.

Content-Independent Concepts and Affect

We can ask a child, "What color is this?" and present an ugly brown spider. Let's say the child responds correctly. We then ask, "Do you like this?" He informs us that he does not. The demonstration object is an instance of *spider, living thing,* etc. It is an instance of brown. Finally, it is an instance of *Something a child does not like.* When the child indicates that he does not like the object, he is not making the same kind of judgement he makes when he says that the object is brown or a spider. Judgements about the spider and brown are based on the characteristics that the object shares with other objects. The judgement about not liking the object, however, is a judgement about the child's reaction to the object. The child is indicating that he reacts to things with certain characteristics by avoiding them.

The basic principle of behavior is that a child tends to do things that he "likes" and tends to avoid things that he doesn't "like." We cannot observe his "liking" or "disliking" any more than we can observe his concept of brown. We discover whether or not he "likes" something by noting his reaction to that object or event. If he acts as if he likes it by approaching the object or event, we conclude that he likes it. He demonstrates that he prefers it over other objects and events. If he tends to avoid an object or event, we conclude that he does not "like" it.

The problem posed by the principle that the child responds "positively" to certain stimulus situations and "negatively" to others is that we must program content-independent concepts on two levels. We must teach the child the rule that governs the pay-off. For example, we must teach him that "If you do X, you will get pay-off Y." However, unless Y is actually an effective reinforcer, the child will not perform in the way that we want. He may know the rule, just as he may know that the brown object we presented is a spider; however, he may react to our demonstration in the same way he reacts to the spider. "I want to avoid it." A pay-off is not something that we *think* should be a pay-off. It is something to which the child *reacts* positively. Unless the child experiences an instance of a real pay-off for doing X, the concept, "If you do X, you will get pay-off Y," does not imply that there is any reason for doing X.

Reinforcers in the Concept Demonstration

In the introduction to this chapter, we noted that reinforcers are used in two different ways in a teaching presentation. They are used non-contingently to maintain interest in the concept demonstrations, and they are used contingently to insure that the child will produce on-task behavior. First, we will discuss the use of reinforcement in the concept demonstration.

Children enjoy watching certain types of objects. They like to listen to certain sound patterns. They react favorably to certain story themes. If a teaching presentation contains elements that children respond to positively, the chances of the child learning to like that presentation are increased, because the teaching demonstration has "pleasurable" characteristics. As noted earlier it is possible to construct a presentation that involves such strong reinforcers that the children have difficulty attending to the salient characteristics of the concept presentation. The stronger the non-contingent reinforcers the greater the possibility that the child will attend to those characteristics of the presentation that *relate to him,* without attending to the concept characteristics that are shared by the instances. For example, we may give a child an ice cream cone and then try to teach the concept cold. The pleasurable characteristic of the ice cream cone may be so strong that the child fails to attend to our presentation. While he may attend to how the ice cream cone "feels," he may have difficulty attending to our presentation of cold.

On the other hand if a presentation is void of strong, non-contingent reinforcers, the teacher will probably find it relatively difficult to maintain attention. Her presentation has no suspense. The child knows all too well what will happen. The teacher will talk. What she says will not be particularly pleasurable—no unique inflections, funny themes, rhymes, etc. There will be nothing to wonder about, nothing new to see. The child, understandably, may not be too eager to become involved in such a presentation.

A dynamic presentation is far more likely to capture and hold its attention. While there are no contingencies in such a presentation, there is a great deal of suspense. The teacher does not present all of the examples at once. She presents them one at a time. The display changes constantly. With every change, the child has something new to see. The teacher uses fun examples and themes. "Okay, this is a story about John. John started out with five teeth. He went to sleep and when he woke up, what do you think happened? He grew nine more teeth. Wow! How many teeth did he end up with?"

A dynamic presentation also involves inflections and rhythms that the children enjoy. "I can say it. The broom is ooover the floor. Clap, clap. The broom is ooover the floor. Say it with me . . ." Finally, the dynamic presentation involves a rather dramatic change of pace. The teacher may talk loudly one time and softly the next. She may move to the next task without any preamble. She may stop in the middle of a presentation and sit without saying a word for a few moments.

The secret to a dynamic presentation is that *the presentation should be relatively unpredictable between routines and very predictable within routines.* Also, the amount of time spent on a particular example should be reduced to the minimum. If the teacher finds herself working on the same example for a few minutes, her presentation has lost a great deal of its dynamic potential. Ideally, the display the children are watching should change at least every minute. Within a routine (which is predictable) unique inflections and examples that interest the children should be employed to maintain interest.

While it is possible to control children's behavior in a presentation simply by using contingent reinforcements (providing pay-offs only if the children behave in the appropriate way), non-contingent reinforcers are important to any program, even if they do not particularly facilitate the learning of the specific content concepts that are being taught. They are important because they provide instances of the concept, "Learning is fun," or, "Arithmetic problems are interesting."

On the other hand, it is often possible to assure adequate task performance simply by programming non-contingent reinforcement. An efficient program, however, contains both—the non-contingent reinforcers to demonstrate that there are pleasurable instances of new learning and the contingent reinforcers to teach the content-independent concepts we wish to program.

Teaching the Children to Like "Neutral" Presentations

We can teach children to "like" a neutral presentation by introducing a routine in which the new stimulus or event is treated in the same way as a known set of reinforcers. For example, we may want a child to respond positively to social praise. The basic requirement of a successful routine is to demonstrate that praise has the same characteristics as a known reinforcer. If we want the child to react to praise in the same positive manner that he reacts to candy, we would demonstrate to the child that praise and candy are used interchangeably, that we process both with the same routine. We first demonstrate a rule of the form, "If you do X, you get the reward." We then show that the reward consists of either praise, candy, or both praise and candy. It is generally assumed that the praise and candy must be presented in a fixed order (praise first and then candy) but this assumption seems highly questionable. The primary requirement is that both praise and candy are treated in the same way. The child then learns the concept that both praise and candy share a set of characteristics. Both function as pay-offs. When the child learns this concept he does not learn that candy and praise are identical. He does not try to eat praise or savor it in his mouth. He learns simply that it has the same function in the presentation as the candy.

An obvious example of how routines affect one's perception of an object can be demonstrated with such neutral objects as worms. They are not associated with stinging, shocks, or other strong, unpleasant stimuli. Yet, we can teach children to react negatively to worms simply be demonstrating that we react to them in the same manner that we react to other repulsive objects. The routine implies that if we treat worms in the same way we treat other objects that have repulsive characteristics, worms must have repulsive characteristics. On the other hand, if we treat worms as amusing objects, we are implying that they have the same set of characteristics as amusing objects.

In the classroom, young children can be taught that examples are funny if the teacher treats them in the same way she would treat things that are funny. If she laughs and makes unique comments about why the example is funny, the children will tend to treat the example as if it is funny. Similarly, if the teacher presents something as if it is interesting, perhaps telling the children that it is interesting, the children will probably exhibit greater interest in the example.

Since it is possible to teach children to react to neutral stimuli as if they are not neutral, it is possible, within limits, to program the type of reaction that the teacher wants to the material. It is possible to "create" non-contingent reinforcers. If she wants the children to think that arithmetic problems are fun, she can act as if arithmetic problems have some of the same characteristics that are shared by fun events, and she can treat the problems as if they are fun.

If an object has strong sensory characteristics that are incompatible with the characteristics we want to teach, the teaching is far more difficult because the child is receiving information contrary to what we are trying to convey through our routine. We are trying to show the child that the object has certain characteristics, and he is receiving information that it does not have these characteristics. For example, we may try to demonstrate that receiving electric shocks is great fun. We may present a number of demonstrations of how much we enjoy being shocked and how we treat this activity just as we would treat any other thoroughly enjoyable experience. The child may not learn to treat an electric shock as fun because the shocks do not have the characteristics we imply they have. We would have a much greater possibility of success if we started with a relatively neutral object. The child would then receive no contradictory information.

Programming Contingent Reinforcers

The use of contingent reinforcement in teaching programs is based on the assumption that some of the requirements placed on the child during new learning are punishing. He does not do them out of choice. He often would rather not behave in the manner that is implied by the task. Despite our efforts to make the presentation more dynamic and interesting, the child may not choose to attend or perform the operations called for. We, therefore, have to demonstrate that the behavior that is called for by the task is actually more rewarding than the other types of behavior.

There are two ways that we can go about teaching the child to like doing what we want him to do. The first is to make off-task behavior more punishing than on-task behavior. If the on-task responses are the only responses that are not punished, the child will produce the on-task responses. The off-task response now have an unpleasant characteristic — they lead to punishment. The on-task responses do not lead to punishment.

We can exaggerate the difference between off-task responses and on-task responses by punishing off-task responses and rewarding on-task responses. The cost of on-task responses is now far less than the cost of off-task responses. Still a third way to teach the child that on-task responses have a "pleasant characteristic" is to ignore the inappropriate responses and reinforce the appropriate ones. This approach has some advantage over the other approaches. The child is given a choice, at least apparently. He can select between behaviors that have moderate reinforcing characteristics and behaviors that have stronger reinforcing characteristics. He makes the choice because he is moving toward a goal—because he wants that pay-off —not because he is trying to avoid unpleasant consequences. A child who is not "coerced" into responding in a certain way has not learned a false rule about the characteristics of the behavior that he has abandoned. He knows that the abandoned behavior is reinforcing and leads to pleasant consequences. He has not received demonstrations that the behavior is painful and should be avoided in the way that one avoids a shock. The behavior should be avoided because it does not lead to a more pleasant pay-off.

Strength of Reinforcers

If we counteract the punishment that is inherent in the response with a strong enough pay-off, the child will learn to respond appropriately. Some reinforcers are not strong enough to counteract the punishment inherent in any but a few tasks. As the response cost of the task goes up (the amount of punishment or unpleasantness of the task) these reinforcers no longer work. Stronger reinforcers must be introduced. The child may not want to learn to tie his shoe when only social praise is offered. The response cost is too great for the pay-off. If we introduce a stronger pay-off, however, (such as receiving a special treat) the child may now be willing to learn to tie his shoe. We have given the process of learning to tie shoes a more pleasant characteristic. It leads to something that the child is willing to work for.

No assumption should be made about the cost of a particular response in a particular situation. One time the response cost of the task may be very high for a child and the next time it may be relatively low. If it is relatively low, only mild reinforcers are needed to assure on-task performance. If it is relatively great, a relatively strong reinforcer is needed. During a session, the response cost may change. The child may become satiated. He may tire. He may find something else in the environment that is more reinforcing than the task. When this happens, a stronger reinforcer must be introduced. The judgement is made on the basis of the child's behavior. If it is evident from his behavior that he is no longer willing to exhibit the kind of behavior that is needed to receive a pay-off, the pay-off should be changed.

This is not to say that the child's failure to respond appropriately is always a function of reinforcement. If this were the case, we could present the strongest possible reinforcer and give him a problem in calculus. He would solve it appropriately. Obviously, the child's ability to produce correct responses is a function of the material— the demonstrations and the tasks. However, his *on-task behavior* (his attempts to work the tasks) is controlled by reinforcers. This distinction is important. If it is ignored, poor programs are sometimes created.

If the child has learned that failing tasks has unpleasant characteristics (leads to unpleasant consequences), a program that has a high failure rate increases the amount of punishment that the child must endure before receiving pay-offs. We can reduce the number of failures by restructuring the tasks, thereby reducing the amount of punishment, or we can introduce stronger reinforcers. The former technique has many advantages over the latter, especially from the standpoint of learning. When a child learns misrules, a more elaborate program is implied, and remedial steps must be taken to contradict his misrule. High failure rate is a good indication that misrules are being induced.

The procedure for teaching children that a particular type of behavior leads to an effective reinforcer is to make the reinforcer contingent upon desired performance. If the child performs in the desired way, he gets the pay-off; if not, he does not get it. After the child has learned to work for a particular pay-off, it is possible to teach the child to work for other pay-offs simply by treating a new pay-off as if it has the same functional characteristics as the original. "If you do this job, I'm going to let you work your arithmetic sheet. How about that?" This approach is similar to the one Tom Sawyer used to convince his friends that whitewashing a fence is the supreme reinforcing activity.

Programming Content-Independent Concepts

We want the child to learn the most productive attitudes about his relationship with learning and performance in the classroom. We want him to learn persistence, to have a positive image of what he can do in the new learning situation. We want him to find pleasure in learning and in using what has been taught. We want him to learn that he should use what has been taught. These are concepts; however, all the programs for each of these concepts involve showing the child that new-learning situations have certain characteristics. The demonstrations cannot be made effectively unless these characteristics are programmed into the *new-learning situations*.

The method for teaching these concepts is similar to that for any concept. Concept instances are presented. The child's attention is called to the salient characteristics of each instance. If possible a verbal rule is introduced to describe all of the instances that will be encountered. A routine is introduced so that instances that have the same set of characteristics can be treated in the same way. All instances are structured so that their characteristic is relatively obvious. Initially, the "pay-off" should be quite obvious. Later, it can be faded. The teacher continues to treat tasks and demonstrations in which the pay-off has been faded in the same way that she had originally treated the tasks with the obvious reinforcing characteristics. The routine prompts the generalization that if they are treated in the same way, they must have the same characteristics. The prophecy is self-fulfilling. If a child treats something as if it is reinforcing, it is reinforcing.

Although these programs hinge on the effective use of reinforcers, they do not derive from behavioral analysis. They derive from concept analysis. In many respects, this statement is trivial, since the same set of conclusions would often be treated by working from behavioral principle. However, as we will see, true differences in programming do result from the concept-analysis approach.

Demonstrating the Concept That What Is Learned Is Used

One of the characteristics about new-learning situations that we want children to feel is that what is learned in the new-learning situation is used in other situations. If the child learns this concept he will tend to rehearse the content concepts he has learned, which means that the chances that he can use the skill in a given task situation is increased. He will classify the skill not as something that is to be parroted back in sterile situations but something that will be of use in a range of situations.

Teaching requirements are imposed by the concept. Ideally we should construct every new-learning situation so that what is learned is used in other situations. The first step is to introduce very obvious instances, in which the delay between learning and using is very short and the application of what has been learned is quite similar to the original learning. A routine is established that will allow us to describe all of the instances that are to be presented—even those that are less obvious than those in the initial demonstration set.

The teacher may begin by first teaching a basic skill, then presenting tasks in which the child can receive the pay-off only if he uses the newly-learned skill appropriately. For example, she may teach number identification. She may then tell the children, "Read the numeral and I'll give you that many raisins. If the numeral is four, you get four raisins. If the numeral is seven, you get seven raisins. Tell me the numeral and you get the raisins." This task should not be presented until the children have demonstrated a mastery of the numerals that are to be presented. Note that the task is an arithmetic task. It is relatively closely related to the original task. As the children respond, the teacher relates each child's performance to the general rule that she is trying to establish. "Good work, John. He remembered that four because he knew that he would use it. And look what he gets for using it—four raisins."

The teacher next begins to introduce the newly-learned skill "out of context." In the middle of a language or science lesson, she presents a number and asks the children to identify it. Again, she relates each child's performance to the rule. "He knew it. He remembered it because he knew that he would use it. Good boy." From time to time the teacher points out that the children can perform complex operations because they have learned basic components. "You can't do this problem unless you know this numeral. What numeral is it? . . . Good. See? You always use what you learn, don't you?"

The program that effectively teaches the concept that what is learned is used contains many content rules. When the program is rule-oriented, the child learns very quickly that the rule is the key for handling a great many problems. "Here's the rule, and it's a good one. Learn this rule and you'll really be able to use it . . ." Every time the child applies the rule, his performance can be related to the concept about using what is learned. "He knows how to use his rules. He knows that you always use what you learn."

The emphasis on rules not only provides a greater range of concept instances but teaches the child a more systematic attack to new learning. Learn the rule and you don't have to worry about memorizing each instance of the rule.

Programming the Concept of Persistence

Persistence is particularly important in a new learning situation. If the child has not been taught that persistence pays off, or stated differently, if the child has not been shown that he can succeed in new learning situations, he will interpret his new learning attempts differently than a child who has been taught that persistence pays off. The new-learning situation is ambiguous. Children will probably not learn without first making some errors. A child who has not been taught that he will succeed if he continues to try will tend to interpret his first frustration as proof that he cannot succeed. "I knew I couldn't do it." He then gives up. His rule is reinforced. He knew he could not succeed, and he did not succeed. The child who has been taught that persistence pays off views the failure in a different way. "I didn't do it this time, but I'll succeed if I keep working." He keeps working and succeeds. The success reinforces his premise. "I knew that if I kept working hard I would succeed." Since both the positive and negative premises are self-fulfilling, it is extremely important to teach children the persistence concept.

Note that both the persistence concept and the concept about using what is learned affect the output of the child. The child who has not been taught the importance of using what is learned may not note how often what is learned is used. And he, therefore, may not make a concerted effort to use what is learned. His output is affected. Similarly, the child who has not been taught that he can succeed if he persists, may not discover the value of persistence. His output is potentially reduced. *All content-independent concepts affect one's output in new-learning and the application of what is learned.*

The program for teaching persistence is implied by the concept that we want to teach. We want to demonstrate that success follows errors in new learning situations. We must demonstrate this concept in connection with every new-learning situation that poses problems for the child. We must show that every troublesome new learning situation has a characteristic: if you persist you'll succeed. Our routine must demonstrate that all of these new-learning situations share the characteristic. Furthermore, we must use effective reinforcement so that the child wants to succeed.

To program persistence, the teacher introduces a statement routine every time one of the children in the group is having difficulty. "Tommy's working hard. You watch. He's going to catch on. If you work hard you'll get it. One of these days he's going to come in here and you'll see. He'll know this stuff. He's a smart boy." The teacher introduces the same routine if one of the other children in the group makes fun of the child who is having trouble. "Wait a minute. He's working hard. And he's going to show you. He'll get this stuff. You'll see."

When the child demonstrates that he has finally mastered the skill, the teacher relates his performance to the rule. She triumphantly announces, "What did I tell you? I told you he would get it. He kept working and working and now he's got it. He's a smart boy. He knows that if you work hard you'll get it. Don't you, Tommy? . . ."

It is very important to relate the child's performance to the verbal rule. The teacher must demonstrate that the other children in the group and Tommy have witnessed an instance of the rule, "If you work hard, you'll get it." She should make sure that she provides adequate recompense for persistence. She does this by making a fuss about the child's new accomplishments, which means that she uses a variation of a routine that signals great excitement. The teacher may also provide the child with some kind of tangible reinforcer. Tangibles (candy, special privileges, etc.) are particularly effective for children who have not had a great deal of experience with learning from adults in a formal situation. For the more sophisticated child, these are often not necessary.

A persistence program should be geared so that a child does not encounter a great deal of frustration in new-learning. The greater the amount of frustration, the greater the cost of working hard and the less frequently the child receives reinforcement for appropriate responses. The program should be geared so that the child can work on four or five skills during a period and possibly encounter difficulty with only one of these. After the child has received a number of demonstrations that he is smart and can succeed if he works hard, the ratio of potential troublesome tasks to errorless tasks can be increased, but not greatly. If the work becomes too hard, the child is quite reasonable in concluding, "It's not worth the pay-off."

Programming a Positive Self-Image

There is no way through a school program that we can teach the child to have an over-all positive self-image. A person's self-image relates to particular classes of activities. A child may feel very confident in the new learning situation and very comfortable in school. At the same time, he may feel quite inadequate at home or with his peers on the playground. The sphere of self-confidence that can be programmed in the classroom has to do with the child's ability to "stick to his guns," to have confidence in what he has learned, and to approach school tasks with the understanding that he is smart and will succeed. For a child to maintain such an impression of himself, he must receive *demonstrations* that these descriptions of himself are *valid*. If he finds himself failing in school, displeasing the teacher, feeling unsure about what he has learned, he must re-evaluate himself and perhaps conclude that he is not a complete success.

A program that is geared so that the child has relatively few learning complications ensures that the child will receive demonstrations that he is smart and capable. Through the programming of the persistence concept and the concept of using what is learned, the child may be taught confidence, but additional steps should be taken to ensure that the child is confident about using what has been learned.

The program begins with simple "fooler" games. The teacher indicates that she is going to "catch" the children unless they are careful. She then announces that she will do something. "I'm going to name animals. Listen: tiger, elephant, dog, table, horse . . ." If the children do not react, she acts gleeful. "I tricked you. Ho, ho. Lisa thinks that a table is an animal. Tyrone thinks that a table is an animal. That's silly." When the children catch the teacher's mistake, she presents the confidence routine. "Good thinking. He knew what was right, and I couldn't fool him by saying something else."

As the children become familiar with a variety of fooler games, the teacher begins to introduce foolers out of context. She is careful never to introduce foolers in the presentation of a new concept, because she wants the children to "trust" her in these situations. However, after the children have mastered a basic skill, such as adding, the teacher may ask the children, "What's six plus two? . . . Yes, eight." She then writes on the board, $6 + 2 = 9$. If the children don't catch the mistake, she acts amused. If they do catch it, she presents the confidence routine. "They *know* what is right and you can't fool them."

Note that these tasks are also good for programming attention. If a child fails the task because he fails to attend, the teacher can point out the importance of attention. "If you don't watch and listen, I'll catch you every time. You don't have to watch and listen, because I like to fool you . . ."

After the children have begun to work with foolers, the teacher can introduce a variation. "I'm going to teach you something that is really hard, and you're not going to be able to get it. I'm the only one who can do it. I'm going to catch you." The teacher then presents a new concept that will probably be learned with little difficulty. The teacher acts surprised. "How did you do that? I thought I could catch you, but I couldn't. You learned this stuff the right way and I couldn't fool you. You're too smart for me." The routine provides the children with a demonstration that if they attack new learning "the right way" they will succeed, even beyond the expectations of the teacher.

For a fooler program to succeed, the material must be carefully sequenced so that the children receive an adequate number of demonstrations that they can be confident about their ability. If they consistently fail in tasks that are billed as tasks they will fail, the demonstrations are not instances of the concept we wish to teach.

Programming Acceptable Classroom Behavior

There are rules of appropriate behavior that should be taught to the children. The most effective technique is to provide a general, verbal rule, that describes all of the instances, and then to demonstrate that the rule holds in the various instances encountered. If the rule holds for situations 1, 2, 3, 4, 5, 6, 7, . . . it should hold for every situation. The rule is useful. The verbal rule without demonstrations is not sufficient to teach the appropriate behavior. If the teacher tells the children a rule about sitting during a seat-work period and then does not enforce the rule, she is providing a demonstration that the rule is hollow. It is possible to teach the rule (or concept) without ever presenting a verbal rule. The teacher can apply the rule consistently and the children will soon learn it. The presentation involving a verbal rule has certain advantages over a no-rule presentation.

1. The rule allows the teacher to specify the salient characteristics of a number of situations that differ in many accidental respects. It, therefore, implies faster learning.

2. The rule allows the teacher to relate the child's performance to a standard. When a child is reinforced for following the rule, the teacher can specify why his behavior is consistent with the rule.

3. The rule allows the teacher to signal the instance of the rule in a way that is consistent with the structure of other verbal rules. "If you do this, something will happen. You did this. There-

fore, . . . " If the rule is demonstrated but not expressed verbally, the child may not clearly see the relationship that the present rule has to other rules and to the general form of if-then (or contingency) rules.

Teaching behavioral rules involves an analysis of the concept that is to be taught. If we want the child to remain in his seat during a particular period, a positive instance of the concept is "sitting in one's seat during the entire period." Negative instances are those in which the child does not sit in his seat during the entire period. The program involves teaching the rule and then demonstrating that the pay-off for sitting in one's seat during the entire period is greater than the pay-off for violating the rule. Each positive instance of the concept has the characteristic that it is followed by a strong, positive reinforcement. Each negative instance of the concept has the charasteristic of being followed by a lack of reinforcer and perhaps punishment.

The most efficient procedure for teaching verbal children is to establish a verbal routine that will cover all of the instances of the concept. "If you sit in your seat for the whole period, I'll give you some bubble gum. If you don't sit, no bubble gum." Initially, the "periods'" may be made relatively short, to decrease the amount of punishment or the response cost of sitting. Also, during the period, there should be an attempt to give the child something relatively easy to do.

In executing the rule, the teacher should first question the child to make sure that he understands the rule. Perhaps she will have to demonstrate the rule, using another child as a shill or model. She should make the reinforcer as attractive as possible, by reacting to it as she would react to very attractive reinforcers. "Oh boy. All you have to do to get this bubble gum is sit in your seat. Are you ever lucky."

The rule should then be scrupulously enforced. If the child stands during the period, the teacher should relate his performance to the rule and inform him that he will not get the pay-off. "If you sit during the whole period, you get the bubble gum. But you did not sit for the whole period. So you don't get the bubble gum. I do." The next day the teacher may introduce a stronger reinforcer, perhaps two pieces of bubble gum, perhaps a piece of bubble gum that is added for every two minutes of appropriate behavior—but none given if the child stands up.

When the child succeeds, the teacher should relate his performance to the rule. "Good boy. If you sit for the whole period, what happens? . . . And here it is. You did a good job."

The procedures for handling any behavior problem are basically the same.

1. The rule is stated. The child is questioned to determine that he understands the rule. If necessary the rule is demonstrated.

2. The consequences that will follow acceptable and unacceptable behavior are clearly specified. The child is told what kind of reward he will receive for complying with the rule and what kind of deprivation or punishment will result if he does not follow the rule.

3. The strength of the reinforcer is increased as the teacher finds it necessary to counterbalance the amount of punishment that the child will have to endure before receiving the pay-off.

4. The child's performance is related to the rule. The rule covers the instances of the concept. If the child's behavior is not consistent with the positive instances, he is told that he did not comply with the rule. "What's the rule? . . . Did you do what the rule says? . . . So are you going to get the bubble gum? . . ." The concept must be demonstrated in the same way that other concepts are demonstrated. Every situation with certain characteristics is followed by a pay-off (or signalled in a certain way). This is an instance of a situation with these characteristics. Therefore, the pay-off follows.

5. The rule must be strictly enforced. Without strict enforcement, the child is shown that the rule does not actually cover the instances it is supposed to cover. The rule, therefore, can be ignored. It cannot be used to predict outcomes. If the rule is strictly enforced, the child learns very quickly that it will hold for all instances. Furthermore, he will learn a form that transfers to other rules. If it is true that rule 1 and rule 2 are strictly enforced, it follows that a new rule, rule 3, will also be strictly enforced. The child does not have to experiment with each new rule that is presented. The teacher's consistent routine demonstrates that all of her rules have the same enforcement characteristic.

CHAPTER VIII

SUMMARY OF THE OUTLINE

A teaching demonstration is a complex admixture of art, psychology and analysis. A single teaching demonstration often can succeed only if it satisfies a number of teaching requirements. It must demonstrate the structure of a specific concept. It must provide a model for the type of responses that will be called for in the tasks. It must contain tasks to provide the teacher with feedback about the child's progress. It must provide adequate recompense for responses (including attention responses) that are demanded of the child. The teaching demonstration must contain routines for teaching the concept cluster that is being programmed and the counter-independent concepts of working hard, using what is learned, and persisting in the face of failure. Unless adequate routines are established, the program will fail to teach some of the children it has the responsibility of teaching. With adequate teaching, there should be virtually no instructional failures. But to achieve the goal of universal teaching success, we have to analyze what we want to teach. We don't have to analyze children.

Since before the days of Comenius, teaching has been viewed as a mysterious unfolding. And the simplistic principles that are taught in many colleges of education today add little to the axioms and half truths promulgated by Comenius, Pestalozzi, and Rousseau. Recently, however, investigators have begun to look at the principles of teaching in a more scientific, and potentially more productive, way. Behavioral analysis, task analysis, and experimentation in concept formation have allowed us to take a rather bold step forward in developing more effective ways to teach. The folklore of the past clings to us because teaching has strong moral implications. If one can "mold" a child to think in a certain way, how do we know that he will not use this technical knowledge to create monsters And there is the question of nature. Is it natural for children to be taught, or should they be allowed to learn? The modern technology is simply technology. It can be used for evil as well as good. But it can be used for good. We teach chidren whether we intend to teach them or not, whether the setting is "natural" or not. There is an advantage in using techniques that assure better teaching and less failure.

Intuition is perhaps the greatest enemy to the kind of analysis offered in this outline. We tend to feel that the way we learned is the best way and that our "concepts" are the only concepts that should be passed on to young children. Our experiences should be their experiences regardless of how attainable this goal actually is. The intuition that we feel about what we have learned has a negligible role in the development of efficient teaching programs. It is supplanted by the type of creative imagination used to solve problems of design. The designer is told what restrictions are to be placed on his "intuition" and what kind of performance requirements are desired for the finished product. Yes, he expresses his imagination—through his design, not through pores of autism and emotion.

The present outline is neither sufficiently complete nor adequately rigorous. Not all teaching problems have been considered; not all programming decisions have been formalized. Hopefully, however, the outline has provided the reader with an awareness both of the complexity of the concepts we wish to teach and of the logical necessity of analyzing these concepts and translating them into teaching presentations that satisfy the requirements imposed by concepts.